Maria Ballard Holyoke

Violets, Early And Late

Poems

Maria Ballard Holyoke

Violets, Early And Late

Poems

ISBN/EAN: 9783744717564

Printed in Europe, USA, Canada, Australia, Japan

Cover: Foto ©Thomas Meinert / pixelio.de

More available books at **www.hansebooks.com**

Maria Ballard Holyoke.

UNIV. OF CALIF. LIBRARY, LOS ANGELES

VIOLETS,

EARLY AND LATE.

POEMS

BY MARIA BALLARD HOLYOKE.

CHICAGO:
MILLS & SPINING, PUBLISHERS.
1886.

Entered according to Act of Congress, in the year 1886, by
MARIA BALLARD HOLYOKE,
In the Office of the Librarian of Congress, at Washington, D. C.

MILLS & SPINING,
PRINTERS,
84, 86 AND 88 FIFTH AVE.,
CHICAGO.

DEDICATION.

To my kindred by ties of blood or relationship,—to cherished friends, akin by ties of affection and congeniality,—to the several peoples among whom I have labored, as the wife of a pastor, in the precious work of the Gospel ; with whom has been my home until now ; where also these songs sprang into being,—to the great, unforgotten multitudes of hearers and noble co-laborers in the five hundred and fifty towns, from Massachusetts' pines to California's Golden Gate, where I have spoken in behalf of Temperance and Christian work,—and to the public, who may find herein suggestiveness or strains accordant with its thought and feeling, this book is affectionately Dedicated.

At many of your firesides or friendly boards I have sat, and by your ministries been strengthened for life's battle. My heart sings of you, as the shell of the sea.

Some of the earlier verses were written from a sick bed while convalescing ; many while pressed with arduous labors and responsibilities. With more of opportunity, I might have accomplished something more worthy.

Forty-six of these children of my brain have already made their bow to the public through the pages of various magazines and the columns of the secular and religious press—many of them unaccompanied by my name. The kindness of their reception has encouraged me to gather together my stray waifs into a permanent home, adding to them sixty poems, the work of my maturer years, and never before published.

While it is true "we learn in suffering what we teach in song" (and some of these lines were written as with blood-drops, "Two Life Pictures" being composed from a sick-bed, while my babe lay in her coffin, not yet folded away in the grave), I would guard against that which has annoyed other writers with respect to their own productions, namely, the inference that each poem is a fact in the author's life. Such inference is unwarranted.

It is the province of a biographer to narrate facts; of a poet, to picture thoughts and emotions, which may be the fruit either of his intuition, imagination, experience, or observation of others, the only requisite being that they be true to nature and of an elevating tendency.

In listening to the inward voice, it is not always possible to distinguish it from the faint reverberation of some bell of memory. I have sought to bring to the public the songs which first sung themselves in my own soul,— the boquets and knots of flowers which, if less beautiful than many another's, grew in my own little posy-bed, watered and nourished by my care, love and tears.

Little book, companion of many earnest hours, go forth on thy mission in this great world. M. B. H.

2130273

CONTENTS.

THE SINGER'S APOLOGY,	7
AN IDYL OF THE OLD ROOF-TREE,	9
MOTHERHOOD,	11
MIRAGE,	13
MY CREED,	16
AMONG THE NIGHTINGALES,	17
THE BATTLE-CALL,	19
GOLD-SEEKERS,	21
HEAVEN IS HERE,	22
TWO LIFE-PICTURES,	24
THE POETS' SYMPOSIUM,	27
WE DON'T FORGET YOU, DARLING,	37
OUR JEWELS,	39
LIVES THAT ARE POEMS,	40
KEEPSAKES,	41
THE PSALM OF DOGSTAR DAYS,	43
WHAT THE DEWDROP TOLD ME,	45
THE ROMANCE OF A FLUTE,	47
EXPECTATION,	50
EYES OF BLUE,	52
ANGELS OF THE HOME,	53
A TEMPERANCE LYRIC,	56
REFRAIN,	57
WHICH WAY?	58
THE OTHER SIDE,	58
GOOD TIMES,	61
ALMOST HOME,	63
THE FLOWERS,	64
TOKENS OF GOD,	66
MOSSES OF BRIGHT MEMORIES,	67
TO THE OLD STONE-QUARRY,	70
DEEDS,	71
BE STRONG IN VIRTUE AND IN GOD,	72
MOONLIGHT IN WINTER,	73
SUMMER MOONLIGHT,	74
GOD'S WAY,	76
INVOCATION OF WATER,	77
A TEST,	78
OLD AGE,	79
THE VILLAGE BELL,	80
OLD FATHER TIME,	82
WHAT IS LOVE?	84
FOUND AT AN INN,	86
PARTING,	89
FOUR VOICES OF LIFE,	90
GRUMBLE ALLEY AND THANKFUL STREET,	92
THE CHANCE MEETING,	94
THE DREAMER,	95
HER POSTSCRIPT,	98
INTERROGATION,	99
ESTRANGED,	101
SING TO ME NOW OF JESUS,	102
SHIPWRECK,	104

CONTENTS.

UNLOVED,	106
THE MONODY OF DOLOROSA,	108
JACK AND POLLY,	110
VESPER MEMORIES,	112
A LOVER'S REMONSTRANCE,	113
A DAYDREAM ENDED,	115
MOSAIC-WORKERS,	116
A DREAM OF ARCADY,	118
THE SUNDOWN SEA,	120
THEY WATCHED THE SUNSET,	122
REST,	125
THE MOTHER'S TASK,	127
IN MEMORIAM,	129
THE EARLY DEAD,	130
LITTLE EVA,	131
VOICES OF NATURE,	133
BABY GRACE,	135
PET CHARLIE,	137
THE ROBIN BY MY WINDOW,	139
SUSPENSE AND RELIEF,	141
BY THE CRADLE-SIDE,	144
THE SPINSTER,	146
STANZAS INSCRIBED TO A YOUNG LADY,	147
THE DEATH OF THE SECOND-BORN,	150
THE EMPTY NEST,	152
LITTLE BROOMSTICK,	153
AT DUTY'S GATE,	157
GOD'S WORLD,	159
ONE MORE DAY,	162
THE VISITOR BY NIGHT,	163
THE TEST OF POETRY,	166
TWILIGHT MUSINGS,	167
WAITING NEAR THE RIVER,	169
PRESSED FLOWERS FROM THE LAND OF LONG AGO.	
A MOTHER,	173
THE SOUL'S QUEST,	174
DISILLUSION,	175
A SONG OF CHEER,	176
A POET'S HEART,	177
ADIEU,	177
PREMONITION,	178
POEMS OF SPECIAL OCCASIONS :	
REUNION POEM,	181
FOR A GOLDEN WEDDING,	184
COMMEMORATIVE STANZAS,	185
MEMORIAL ODE,	187
LOOKING FORWARD,	188
HARK! THE MUFFLED DRUMS ARE BEATING!	190
PRIZE CARRIER'S ADDRESS, 1859,	192
PRIZE CARRIER'S ADDRESS, 1860,	198
TWENTY-EIGHT,	201
THANKS,	204
TEN CIRCLING YEARS,	205
THE MINISTRY OF GRIEF,	207
THE POET AWAITING A VERDICT,	209
MY BIRDS,	210
VIOLETS,	211

The Singer's Apology.

IF I may not, like the skylark,
    Soar with glorious bursts of song,
Nor, like pensive nightingale,
    Strains most ravishing prolong;

Nor, a little, timid linnet,
    Sweetly gush in hawthorn tree;
If a warbler to entrance you
    I may never, never be;

If to wake the distant echoes
    I have two notes, or but one,—
Be it mourning dove's or cuckoo's,—
    With full soul I will sing on.

God has room for all His creatures,
    And the varied tone of each
Fills the air with richer music
    Than the single silv'rest speech.

Monotones may be full royal;
    Monotones the heart can move;
And the note I'd sing in dying
    Is the golden note of LOVE.

Mother-love—of all most tender,
    Never-dying, ever free;

VIOLETS, EARLY AND LATE.

Lover's love—the most ecstatic;
    Filial love—so sweet to me;

Love of angels hovering o'er us,
    Guiding, guarding us from harm;
Father-love—the great All-Father's,
    Filling us with heavenly calm!

Souls distraught by angry voices,
    Faint with toil, and care-opprest,
Loves of earth or loves of Heaven
    Softly sung may give you rest.

Love shall bring surcease of sorrow,
    Heal the wounds of man's untruth;
Love shall sing of brighter Morrow,
    Or recall the days of Youth,—
    Ring the silver bells of Youth!

An Idyl of the Old Roof-tree.

LONG time a dweller in the town,
    Far from my childhood's peaceful home,
At length I dropped my burdens down,
    A golden month to rest and roam.
The city's din is far away,
    The country's green is at my feet;
The sun of June makes fair the day,
    The meadow's breath is fresh and sweet.
        And at my will
        I saunter still,
Adown the orchard, o'er the hill.

How looms the Past, while here I rove
    And scan my early haunts again!
A child I wander in the grove,
    And echo back the thrush's strain;
Pluck in the wild grass posies gay,—
    Windflowers and bluebells in the woods,—
Snuffing the fragrant new-mown hay,
    Sighting the fawn in solitudes.—
        Noting the tree
        With nestlings three,
Or where the ripe June apples be!

I pause to drink at mossy spring,
    And track the cornfield's vivid green;
I hear again the wild lark sing

From out the wheatfield's golden sheen.
Then seek the leaf-hid mansion, where
 My mother smiles at open door,
And strain to see the silver hair,—
My father's—who will come no more.
   The tears so flow
   I scarcely know
If it be Now or Long Ago!

Oh! dear the old farmhouse to me!
 The homely ways, the ample cheer;
The refuge at my mother's knee
 From childhood's every grief and fear.
And dear the memory of those days,
 Bathed in love's amber atmosphere,
When all our voices rose in praise,
 When sire and child were bowed in prayer.
   But where are they,
   The fond, the gay,
Who filled the great, white house with May?

Gone like the birds from last year's nest!
 Gone as the leaves in autumn fly!
Some to the cities of the West;
 Some toil beneath an Indian sky;
Some, other prairies sow and reap;
 One sank beneath the moaning sea;
Some in the churchyard lie asleep;
 And, quivering in the Old Roof-tree,
   One homesick waits
   The swing of gates
To waft her to Heaven's bright estates!

Motherhood.

I.

O YE who rock the little men,
   Or kiss the cherub on your knee,
I view you with a secret pain,—
   My babes are gone from me.
Your darlings sport in lovelit room,—
   Mine dreamless sleep where violets blow.
Your roof-tree's white with summer bloom,
   But mine is white with snow!
   Ah! with untimely snow.

II.

O homes that ring with childhood's mirth!
   O happy bosoms babies press!
Ye may not know how drear is earth
   Without a child's caress.
When, tiring of the wee ones' calls,
   You long to flee from strife and noise,
Think! some would part with lands and halls
   To have their girls and boys,—
   Those long-lost girls and boys!

III.

Madonna and the saintly child,
   The artists paint her evermore.
She's the ideal of their dreams,—
   The infant's at their door.

And Paradise comes back to earth,
    And home's a little heaven below,
Where tender, sacred joys have birth,
    Which only parents know;
    Ah! happy parents know!

IV.

True Motherhood is most like God.
    True Motherhood is of the soul;
Heeds not the sensuous tie of blood,
    Loves not with scanty dole.
Forgets not, though the seas divide,
    And separating years be long;
Though locks grow blanched and faith be tried,
    True Motherhood is strong,—
    Is deep, and pure, and strong.

V.

Some great hearts, too, by God's strange chrism
    Such majesty of love attain,
They leap across Sin's dark abysm,
    To clasp a race of men.
Woman may feed the altar-fires,
    Fair priestess of a hallowed home,
Or walk where purity expires,
    To guide the feet that roam;
    (O feet, how far ye roam!)

VI.

Or lift the drunkard up from wrong,
    Or sit sweet teacher of the youth,
Or tell a hushed and waiting throng
    The wonders of God's truth.

MIRAGE.

In all, her Mother-heart's the same;
To love and service consecrate;
Fidelity her constant aim,—
    Her crown at Heaven's gate,—
    Crowned at the jasper gate!

Mirage.

I.

NOON on the burning sands!
    The desert stretched its somber waste around.
Afar, the gloomy, rock-ribbed mountains frowned,
And, as with savage guards, the vast plain bound.
    Slow paced the caravans.
The sun shot down his blistering, golden fire,
And tree was none, to shelter from his ire.

II.

    'Water! I parch with thirst.
O for a cooling drink!' one moaning cried—
'One long, sweet draught, kneeling by fountain side!
O but to lave, to plash, in flowing tide,
    While in this land accurst!
To bathe refreshingly this fevered brow!
A streamlet's gush were heavenly music now.

III.

'Would I could stand again
Beside my father's well, and hear the dip
Of mossy bucket in its depths, and sip
Its pure, delicious nectar on my lip,
    And greet my mother, then.
Alas! alas! the good old days are o'er;
I never prized them half enough before.'

IV.

    For days, nor brook, nor bird,
Nor green oasis met the traveler's eye.
On swept the rock waste, streaked with alkali,
And man and beast were fain to sink and die.
    But hark! a shout is heard.
'Water! look yon! a sparkling river flows!
Bear up, speed on! soon we shall end our woes.'

V.

    Joy leaped from eye to eye.
Electric flashed around the blessed news,
And smiling, new-born Hope did swift infuse
Fresh strength into each eager courser's thews.
    They sped right merrily.
Mile after mile of sand, they spun, they flew;
But lo! the long-sought stream no nearer grew!

VI.

    As if a mocking wraith,
Distinct to sight, the blue, blue waters shone,
And, tantalizing, lured the travelers on;
But when approached, all liquid trace was gone.
    Some, gasping, swooned in death.

'T was but a cruel phantasm of the sands—
The weird Mirage that haunts the desert lands.

VII.
Of phantom lights beware!
A haughty soldier seized his gleaming blade.
'I fight for glory,' proudly thus he said,
Then rushed to gory field, and soon was dead.
    He grasped at empty air.
Not for humanity his deed was done;
Ambition's false Mirage allured him on.

VIII.
    Burning the midnight oil,
A scholar studied, toiled and wrote for fame,
And from its topmost rung inscribed his name;
Drank deep its draught, more thirsty still became—
    Poor recompense for toil.
The millionaire with gold was still unblest.
Mirage of wealth and honor bring no rest.

IX.
'True love, sweet love for me,—
Divine elixir to a woman's heart!'
Thus spake a maiden to herself apart.
O lily soul, beware thy lover's art;
    He fooleth, fooleth thee.
Ere human vows but vain illusion prove,
Know—Heaven yields unfailing love for love.

My Creed.

I HOLD the Fatherhood of God;
    The Brotherhood of Man to man;
My Country's wide as arch of heaven,—
    All people are my countrymen.

I hold that Sin is Selfishness.
    Whose heart is Love is most like God;
He nearest Heaven who lives to bless;
    Himself most blest in doing good.

I hold, as music sweet, one Name,—
    'T is every human name above;
Jesus, the Holy One, who came
    To show the world the Father's love.

He came a light to man in night,
    Revealed the guilt and doom of Sin;
The way to peace and holiness,
    And sweetly drew the wanderers in.

The Soul's an Organ, nobly made;
    But mute or jangling, ah! how soon,
Till, by the Great Musician played,
    'T is gloriously vibrant grown.

Come, Heavenly Lyrist, me attune.
    I need thy touch; sweep all my keys.
Do what thou wilt unto thine own,
    Only evoke thy harmonies.

Among the Nightingales.

I.

FIRST I heard in happy childhood,
    When the rosy day grew pale,
Float from dewy, tangled wildwood
    Thrilling song of Nightingale.
Where the brook was shaded over
    By the tall embracing woods,
There sweet Philomel, the lover,
    Charmed the listening solitudes;
Told her heart amid the gloaming—
    Trilled her passion o'er and o'er;
Gushed in strains that thrilled and filled me,
    And will haunt me evermore.

II.

'Or the years are flitting, flitting!
    I am sitting far away
From the loyal hearts and royal
    Who enfolded me that day.
Hopes have vanished, dreams been banished;
    Burdens must be borne each day.
Help another, foe or brother,
    Is the Law of Love alway.
Open ears I lend to Reason—
    Ponder deeply all her tales.
'Life's a prosy, work-day season'—
    But—I hear my Nightingales.

III.

Love doth ravish as completely
    As the bird of long ago;
Faith and Hope still singing sweetly
    O'er the winter's sleet and snow:
'Truth is Beauty, Love is Duty—
    Love is God, and God is good.'
Chords chromatic grow ecstatic
    When life's tune is understood.
O, though Cold's a bold newcomer—
    Though the Stormwind sails and wails—
Hearts that love have golden summer,
    And they list to Nightingales!

The Battle-Call.

WAKE! wake! wake!
    There's a Demon abroad in the land!
Lo, an enemy's host! hear the War-fiend's blast!
    Rally, each patriot band!

Gather on prairie and glen!
    Muster the East and the West;
March forward, brave men, beard the lion's den;
    Yield to no tyrant's behest.

Be worthy your reverend sires;
    Your cause is the truest and best.
See! Freedom expires! save it and your fires!
    Who bleeds for his country is blest.

  .   .   .   .

They have heard the shrill bugle-blast;
    They have leapt at a nation's loud call;
They have marshal'd in haste, quick partings have pressed;
    They have gone to conquer or fall.

God save 'mid the death-dealing guns
    That valiant, unfaltering host.
They are love's cherished ones, our husbands and sons—
    May they ever, as now, be our boast.

White lips have kissed them farewell,
    And, smiling, sped them away.

But the signal-bell seemed a funeral knell,
And wearily wears the day.

. . . .

Hark! 't is the battle's din,
    The cannon's thundering roar,
The artillery's flash, the deafening crash,
    On fields all covered with gore.

Mown down by hundreds, they lie
    'Neath the batteries' raking fire;
But still the cry, "The foe, they fly!"
    Urges the conflict dire.

Intrepid souls, in vain!
    Tomorrow's sun shall see
The stiffened slain, o'er all the plain,
    Nor yours the victory.

Wail, bitterly wail,
    For the gallant, early dead.
The sod shall be their sepulcher,
    The battle-field their bed.

Yet, undismayed, arise,
    My country, for the fight.
If thy flag waves o'er chatteled slaves,
    Thou go'st not forth aright.

Strike off Oppression's chain!
    Dare nobly to do right!
Heaven shall forefend, and triumph send
    The hosts of God's own might.

September, 1861.

Gold-Seekers.

I.

'TWAS in the sundown hunting-grounds of gold,
    Near where the white Sierras pierce the skies;
Where once, o'er ruddy treasures, rivers rolled,
    And miners shrilled Eureka! with glad cries,
    And, flushed with sudden wealth, bore off their prize.

II.

Long since, the great Bonanza is no more;
    The ancient camping-grounds are desolate.
Adventurous Yankees seek some other shore,
    Where for their greed more tempting fortunes wait.
    The miners' huts stand lonesome, mocked of Fate.

III.

'T was from a mountain side I caught a gleam
    Of river winding through those barren lands.
One lone "Celestial" stood within the stream,
    And shook a miner's pan in his worn hands,
    Content by toil to glean a few gold sands.

IV.

O weary, bravely patient Chinaman!
    Who, coming to an oft-worked field so late,
Still gathers up what yellow dust he can

Where others heaped their yellow nuggets great.
Yet he, as they, has helped enrich the State.

V.

I'm a Gold-Seeker in the mines of Truth.
I toil amid the hurrying waves of Time.
Thought-land was worked by masters ere my youth.
May one so weak, so late, find golden rhyme,
And make the song-world richer for my chime?

Heaven is Here.

Last words of Mrs. H. W. S., of Polo.

A SAINT lay dying on her bed;
Departing, felt no fear.
"Heaven is coming," she sweetly said—
Then quickly, "Heaven is here!"

O rapturous thought! exceeding joy!
O glory dimly guessed!
Did angel companies convoy
Your spirit to the Blest?

HEAVEN IS HERE.

Perhaps, the film of sense withdrawn,
    You saw the City of Light;
The golden harpers by the Throne,
    The saved ones robed in white.

Perhaps this other truth was given:
    That all who heavenward go,
The purified, the sin-forgiven,
    Begin their Heaven below.

Who, as himself, holds others dear—
    Whose heart's by Love possessed—
Dwells *here* in upper atmosphere,
    And is divinely blest.

Heaven lies around the holy soul.
    Faith calms his anxious fears;
Faith makes the wounded spirit whole,
    Or jewels e'en his tears.

Within the heart that kingdom lies.
    O thought of blessed cheer!
O mystery of mysteries!
    We may have Heaven here!

Two Life-Pictures.

I. BABY MAY.

SIX years since we were wedded, love,
    Have gone this very day;
'T was in the pleasant wooing-time
    Of bright and balmy May.

Our hearts are still as warm as when
    We breath'd that solemn vow;
I thought I loved thee fondly then,—
    I know I love thee now!

Today our cherub child has come:
    This baby girl is given
To be the jewel of our home,
    Its sunbeam fresh from Heaven.

She is our pretty, only bird,—
    She is our first-born child.
What wonder if our souls are stirred
    With raptures new and wild?

She has her father's thoughful brow,
    Dark eyes and soft brown hair,
A loving little mouth and chin,—
    Our May is sweet and fair.

A spirit her young bosom fills:
    Be it our constant care.

'T will vibrate with a thousand thrills—
  God's image may it bear!

A trust so holy and so great
  We take with trembling joy.
Our precious child we consecrate
  To Christ and His employ.

And when, 'mid future toil and strife,
  We yearning sigh for rest,
Still beautiful will be our life
  With her dear presence blest.

Light of the house! sweet rose of May!
  Love's dower long delayed'
Never such bliss our bosoms thrilled
  As that which thou hast made!

II. ANGEL MAY.

Solemnly pause on the silent threshold,
  Softly tread o'er the darkened way;
Yonder she lies in her coffin reposing,
  The child of our love,—our heart's darling May!

Mute is the air,—save with wailing of mourners;
  Hushed the soft voice,—making music most sweet;
Closed the large eye—the soul's open portal;
  Pallid the brow, and still the heart-beat.

Slight baby hands white rosebuds are clasping;
  None of earth's flowers were lovely as she.
Sweet was the grace of our frail budding blossom—
  What will our full rose in Paradise be?

VIOLETS, EARLY AND LATE.

Make her a grave 'neath the soft summer greensward,
    Tenderly bear our best treasure away;
Precious the dust that enshrined the immortal
    Who rests in the bosom of Jesus today.

She was the star in affection's horizon,
    Our comfort, our blessing, our innocent dove;
She was an angel that shone on our dwelling,
    Then plumed her white pinions for regions above.

Oh! dark grows the day, and the roof-tree is dreary,
    Where home joys the sweetest but lately had birth;
Oh! dull grows the earth, and our hearts are aweary—
    Child! child! thou hast left this a desolate earth!

Yet, sweet one, thy memory shrined on Love's altar
    Sacred and beautiful ever shall be;
Our gentle rebuker when tempted we falter,
    Our angel approver when evil we flee.

We will still meekly submit to our Father,
    Who planted the bud in His amaranth bower,
Patiently trusting that when life is over
    We'll clasp our arms round her, and part nevermore.

The Poets' Symposium.

GENIUS may consort with princes,
    Star in proud palatial halls;
But 't is "to the manner born"
    Of common life and humble walls.

For the Muses love to wander
    Over mountain, over moor;
Haunt the shady dell and fountain,
    Peep in lowly cottage door;

Croon a lullaby o'er cradles,—
    Dance upon the village green;
Sup ambrosia from the flowers,—
    Dream beside the lakelet's sheen;

Plead the suit of rustic lover;
    Sigh in ear of peasant maid;
Chant in cell of hero-martyr,—
    Wind a requiem o'er the dead.

But these soulful, winsome sisters,
    With their glorious gifts of song,
Shrink from clinking vaults and coffers;
    Shun the giddy, heartless throng;

Flee from what is cold and hollow,
    What is artificial, base;

Wooed and won and wed forever
    By true heart and honest face!

Thus the souls of lofty passion—
    Poets blest with goddess' love,—
Quit the garish courts of fashion,
    Deeper, purer joys to prove.

Thus the simpler folk around them
    Breathe the fragrance they distil,
As the vase which long held roses
    Sheds the scent of roses still.

Ah! the least may keep their presence,
    For in books their Authors live!
Books are life-blood, spirit, essence;
    These immortal perfumes give.

    .   .   .   .   .   .

I will paint you a Symposium
    Where with Poets oft I feast.
These are singers ripe and royal,
    And each freely gives his best.

You will find no pomp of riches,
    Gorgeous hangings, lordly hall,
Sculptured Cupids in the niches,
    Masterpieces on the wall,—

Furnishings of stately splendor,
    Air that palls with hothouse bloom,—
This is simple, pure and fragrant,—
    Just "a white rose of a room."

Second story, this sky-parlor,
    Perched above a busy street!
Near to changeful life and motion,
    Where four ways of traffic meet.

Sounds fantastic music making,
    Clang of smithy, puff of train;
Hard by rears a gaunt, grim windmill,
    Swinging round and round again.

In the room's a sweet-toned Steinway,
    Ballads, photos, books, guitar;
Two-score poets on the what-not,
    Open volumes here and there.

Just a cosy, homelike center,
    Such as thousand parlors are;
But to me a glowing Bethel,
    Angels coming down the stair.

Often when I'm stilly sitting,
    Reading o'er th' immortal rhyme,
Soul to soul I hear them, speaking
    Once again, the bards sublime.

Gracious presences seem real;
    Far away Care's surges roar.
I am in a world ideal,
    Lonely, wistful now no more.

Palpitates the air with spirit;
    Sense and self withdraw apart;
Now I feel the throb of ages!
    Clasp the world unto my heart!

Oh, sweet tumult of emotion,
    Trembling, surging in my breast!
Feelings strange, which like an ocean
    Onward sweep and cannot rest.

Poets! ye are charm dispensers;
    Ye have made Enchanted Ground.
Poet-thoughts are burning censers
    Swinging balmy odors round.

Soul of song! the angels love thee,
    Glorious Bird of Paradise.
Lifted on thy free, brave pinions,
    Who aspire may reach the skies.

TRIBUTE TO MRS. E. B. BROWNING.

While I listened to the Singers,
    One awoke a golden song,
Sang of deathless love and duty,
    Sang each true and sang them long.

English skylark, Mrs. Browning,
    Though she held Italia dear;
Trilled "Aurora," "De Profundis,"
    Trilled her "Sonnets" crystal clear,

Sweet as honey. Fondest lover
    Ne'er confessed in tenderer lay.
Over Nature's wildering keyboard
    Flew her hand in skillful play.

None more worthy of the Bay-crown;
    Never nobler soul had breath.

Be her name an inspiration.
On her grave I lay this wreath.

TRIBUTE TO TENNYSON.

Green thy brow with fadeless laurel,
    England's Laureate, Tennyson.
Touch of thine recalls the lyrist
    Who with song did move the stone.

Clear thou seest with prophet vision, —
    Faultless wieldest Fancy's wand.
Driftest us through seas of silver,
    Nigh a music-haunted land.

"In Memoriam"—it voiceth
    All who tender grief have wed.
Locksley Hall's a martial band-burst,
    After happy love has fled.

Of all lofty thought and feeling
    Grand Interpreter art thou.
Madrigal and "Idyl" charm us,
    Sweet as roses, pure as snow.

TRIBUTE TO WORDSWORTH.

First, O philosophic Wordsworth,
    Read I thee in days of youth,
With wide-open eyes, that noted
    Pearls of beauty, gems of truth.

Dear as flowers in childhood gathered,
    Still I hold in Memory's cells
"We are Seven"—"She was a Phantom:"
    Stars of heaven thus shine from wells.

VIOLETS, EARLY AND LATE.

Ministering priest of Nature!
    Though within her heart didst look,
Caught'st her daisy-printed secrets,
    Sung by skylark, gushed by brook;

Golden-writ on evening primrose,—
    Wind-breath'd over woodland fount,
Rural life thou limnest nobly,
    Artist-Seer of Rydal Mount.

TRIBUTE TO BURNS.

Hark! one singeth, heartsome ringeth
    "Auld Lang Syne" and " a' that,"
"The honest man, though e'er sae poor,
    Is king of men for a' that."

Robbie Burns! dear Robbie Burns,
    Stout defender of the lowly!
Each brave thought, each deed well wrought,
    Helps the cause that's pure and holy.

From Bonnie Doon was hushed too soon
    The voice that wooed sweet Highland Mary.
O Scotia! when will bard again
    Wake strains so ravishing and faery?

TRIBUTE TO SHAKSPEARE.

In the galaxy of genius
    Shineth one transcendant star;
Bright, mysterious, commanding,
    In the centuries' Blue afar.

All unite to him reverence,
    All delight to own him king.

THE POETS' SYMPOSIUM.

Shakspeare! universal poet!
  Many spirits in him sing.

By what mother formed and nourished
  Came those great, surpassing powers?
By what teacher trained and tempered
  In his youth's impetuous hours?

Ask the grave! It cannot hear thee.
  Mute as Sphynx on Egypt's sands.
Monument unique and peerless
  Stands the work of Shakspeare's hands.

TRIBUTE TO COLERIDGE.

Many methods had the harpers,
  Grave or jocund, fond or gay;
But the pain, the bliss of loving
  Ever seemed the favorite lay.
Exquisite that strain by Coleridge,
  Heard from tender lips at eve,
How he breathed his fervent passion,
  How he won his "Genevieve."

TRIBUTE TO HOOD.

Twin with Love is Charity.
  When entwined the sisters stand,
One in white and one in crimson,
  Fairer vision hath no land.

Charity's the pure-robed daughter
  Of the great forgiving King.
She was near, inspiring angel,
  When our Hood began to sing.

Genial Hood, whose changeful fancy
    Dimpled like a windswept lake!
Quick and generous his pity
    For the wretched poor, who quake

When the hungry wolf is glaring
    At the open cottage door;
For the erring whom the scornful
    Spread no kindly mantle o'er.

Hood's the poet for the million.
    Who knows not his "Bridge of Sighs?"
Yet he learned in pain the music
    Which with tears has filled our eyes.

TRIBUTE TO MRS. HEMANS.

Fixed in Fame's cerulean,
    Among the stars of England's glory,
Shines serenely Mrs. Hemans,
    After life's untranquil story.

"Breaking waves dashed high" above her,
    Made her song the sadder, sweeter,
Could not dim the poet eyes
    That have vision now completer.

"Answer, burning stars of night!"
    Keeping watch until the morn,
Do no human nightingales
    Sing divine, unpierced by thorn?

  .   .   .   .

In the bright symposium
    Fancy-pictured round my board, —

Thus from Helicon they come,
  And the rare elixir's poured.

Here for thund'rous brows of Genius
  There are thought-illumined Books!
Here the merry feast is Reason!
  And the Poets are the cooks!

Here they lie, all night on bookshelves;
  Never wrangling sound is heard.
You will find no envious mock-elves—
  Generous welcome is assured.

Other poets with the Purple
  Oft the diapason swell:
Dr. Young with praise of Friendship,
  Massey with Babe Christabel;

Dante, loved of Beatricé,
  From Cimmerian darkness led;
Milton awful from Olympus,
  Laurel-wreathed about his head.

In this charmed, magic circle
  From the New World there belong
Bryant, Whittier, Longfellow,
  Grand Triumvirate of Song.

Holland, too, whose bell of silver
  Tolled life's epic, "Bitter Sweet."
Loved of earth and loved of Heaven,
  Aureoles for these are meet.

"When a blow was struck for Freedom,"
When our sky was overcast,
Lowell's crisis-words were drumbeats,
Loudly rang his clarion blast.

In the symphonies of poets
Time would fail me to rehearse
All the robins, finches, thrushes
Heard in cadences of verse.

Sometimes fell amid the pauses
Of the older nightingales,
Sudden gush of limpid pathos,
Deep as when the north wind wails.

Sweet as breath of tuberoses;
(Love, thou wert too sweet to die),—
Then with trills and thrilling closes,
Sudden ceased, and ceased for aye!

Conway, Work, H. H.,—they perished,
When their sun of fame was high.
Shrined in hearts, they will be cherished
With the names not soon to die.

So I dream, amid the gloaming,
Of Arcadia come again,
When the tuneful Nine went roaming,
And the gods conversed with men!

We Don't Forget You, Darling.

WE don't forget you, darling,
    Though many months have flown,
And the turf upon your little grave
    Has green and grassy grown.
The earth has still its summer grace,
    And crowds move thoughtless on;
But O we long for your winsome face,—
    Our dewy rose unblown!

Men dream it oft a trifling wo
    When a young infant dies;
But countless weeping Rachels know
    The soul's deep agonies.
Torn from the trusting babe that lay
    Long nestled near the heart,
Life ever has a vacancy
    Unfilled by human art!

We don't forget you, darling—
    O no, we still are true.
Each frail memento is most dear
    That once was linked with you.
At night, in dreaming slumbers bound,
    You are again our own,—
Again our arms entwine you 'round,—
    We wake, to mourn alone.

VIOLETS, EARLY AND LATE.

Through thee all children seem more fair.
    Sweet sound their tripping feet—
Their birdlike voices on the air—
    Light laughter in the street.
God has ordained that evermore
    Love makes the world akin!
One babe unlocks the heart's wide door,
    That all may enter in!

We don't forget you, darling,
    Safe in the Lovely Land;
Perhaps a crown is on your brow,
    A harp within your hand.
We long again to greet you,
    When earthly toils are done.
O bliss untold, to meet you!
    O joy, when Heaven is won!

Till then we'll ever meekly strive
    Our duties to fulfill;
Teaching the erring how to live,
    Loving our Father's will.
But we won't forget you, darling,
    Though far hence we rove.
You still will be our polar star,
    Pointing to realms above.

Our Jewels.

A MOTHER took the fragile toy,
    Too rich and rare for infant hands,
And kept it for her darling boy,
    Where, though unseen, secure it stands.

Unconscious thus that love was shown,
    The grieving infant wept in pain,
Nor knew when old and wiser grown
    He should receive his own again.

God, like a careful mother, takes
    A treasured jewel of the heart—
A babe, a wife, whose presence makes
    The mighty tides of feeling start.

And we, like children, murmur sore
    When yielding up each precious gem;
Nor think to find, when years are o'er,
    Each link safe in God's diadem!

Lives that are Poems.

SWEET Poesy! thou gift divine,
  Twin sister unto Song!
Love's priceless legacy to man!
  An angel 'mid earth's throng!

Favored are they who know thy spell,
  And wield thy magic wand.
A thousand hearts with rapture thrill,
  Touched by their magic hand.

Yet other souls unknown to Fame
  Have caught the immortal spark.
They wear no Poet's honored name;
  They carve no shining mark.

Theirs is the long and weary night
  Of sorrow and of care;
Keeping the homelight warm and bright —
  No time to string the lyre.

Then deem not that with those alone
  A poet's spirit dwells,
Whose touch awakes the slumbering tone
  From Music's thousand cells.

For other hearts are fraught with song,
  Though heard by mortals never.
Life's Poem they write out in Deeds
  Of love and goodness ever!

Keepsakes.

I.

ONLY a little posy-knot,
   Yet long 't will treasured be,
The first my sprightly laddie brought,
   And smiling gave to me!
He is a bearded man today,
   And has his nestlings three;
But still I see with this boquet
   My Boy—that used to be.

II.

Only a faded, fragrant bloom,
   Recalling orange grove,
Again I bask in sweet perfume,—
   Again by foothills rove:
Or ride beside the sunset sea,
   Where light waves kiss the shore,—
Or float on ocean flowing free,
   And view the old scenes o'er.

III.

Only a faded leaf and flower,
   That with my dead have lain,
Mementoes of a tender hour
   That ne'er will come again.
O baby hands! O snowy brow!
   O sunny rings of hair!

Too beautiful for death wert thou;—
Now, thou art angel fair.

IV.

Only some English violets,
  That caught the sunshine's gold,
And paid in wondrous sweets the debt,—
  These bring the dream of old;
The tender days whose speech is dumb;
  Such hours of pleasure-pain
As some have wished had never come—
  Or else were here again!

V.

Only some letters tied with blue,
  And yellow now with years;
Once christened with the honeydew
  Of kisses and of tears.
The lines still seem electric life,
  As in the days of yore;
The rapture that is felt but once,—
  Alas! if e'er 't is o'er!

The Psalm of Dogstar Days.

The poets string the lyre to sing
The tender beauty of the Spring,—
The splendid grace of Autumn's face,—
Who sings the Psalm of Dogstar Days?

SUMMER'S scorching heats have come.
Springtime's singing-birds are dumb.
Snowy lily, rare-red rose
Perfumed sweets no more disclose.
Droop we in the shady bower,
For the Dogstar rules the hour.

Through the glowing heavens higher
Rides the Sungod's car of fire.
From his eyes shoot burning glances,
Bannered hosts of gleaming lances,
Tipped with flame, that burn their way
All the sweltering Dogstar Day.

Not a moment's cooling breeze!
Not a leaf stirs in the trees!
Nature seems to make a pause;
E'en the hours forget their laws,
Dragging leaden-weighted feet,
Hours that erst were light and fleet.

Fainting, gasping, nigh to death,
Cry we for one cooling breath.

VIOLETS, EARLY AND LATE.

Blow from Northern snows, O gale,—
Touch electric! thee we hail
Kinder friend than tyrant-lover,
Whose hot kisses burn us over.

. . . .

Soul! O soul! art thou aweary
    Of the fever-heat of life?
Fainting with the endless struggle?
    Bruiséd with the needless strife?
In thy secret depths dost moan
'True hearts dead, and false ones flown?'

In thy zodiac of duty
    Rains the Dogstar's baleful fire?
From thy rosebush fall the roses?
    From thy nerveless hand the lyre?
Pantest thou for breath divine,
Re-inspiring life of thine?

Deem not strange the allotted ways.
Whitest souls have saddest days.
All thou feelest is the heat,
    Thee to shape in beauty's mold.
Lo! yon emerald sea of wheat
    Dogdays ripe to sea of gold!

Everywhere one law controls
Realm of sense and realm of souls.
Had there been no blaze of sun,
Harvest-plenty there were none.
Patience! after blinding light
Comes the cool and pleasant night.

August 1, 1885, mercury 98 degrees in the shade

What the Dewdrop Told Me.

O TWINKLING little Dewdrop,
    Slumbering in the rose,
Broidering as with jewels
    Every leaf that grows,

What can a thing so tiny
    Do for the world that's good,
Compared with flashing fountains
    Or the thundering flood?

Think of the deep, broad river,
    Where gallant navies ride!
Behold the sweep of ocean!
    Pray, what are *you* beside?

Then in the purple gloaming
    The answer met my ear,
Sweet as a bell of silver
    Tinkling in crystal sphere.

'The tender, all-wise Father
    Maketh both great and small;
Each has a heaven-born mission,
    A love-work is for all.

'I and my myriad sisters
    Are Nature's nursing-band;

VIOLETS, EARLY AND LATE.

And with unceasing service
　Through the long night we stand.

'The face of earth aweary
　With healing kiss we press,
And all things faint and drooping
　Our silent presence bless.

'I brood all night with flowers,
　Bathing their violet eyes,
Cooling their cheeks' red satin,
　Deep'ning their gorgeous dyes.

'The stars watch in their marches
　Our footprints o'er the green;
Only the daydawn's splendor
　Shows man where we have been.'

'T was still; the full-orb'd sunrise
　With amber glory shone.
The air with life grew ringing,
　The dew exhaled and gone.

Long mused I on its lesson:
　Call nothing mean or small.
Fulfill thy lot, though lowly,
　For God hath use for all.

The Romance of a Flute.

THE moon is scudding through the sky
All in a boat of white,
And making in her starry wake
A firmament of light.

A flood of splendor bathes the world,
And shimmers through the trees,
And music's silver cadences
Come floating on the breeze.

Beside my open casement low
I watch the crimson bars
Of sunset fade to pearly gray,
And wait the shining stars;

And see the landscape fill with light
Bewilderingly fair,
As if some wondrous witchery
Were in the evening air.

Come sit beside me, darling boy,
And lay your palm in mine,
And hear the lovely music float
Upon the sweet moonshine,—

And as you drink the beauty of
The silent evening hour,

VIOLETS, EARLY AND LATE.

Your eyes shall speak the language that
    Your lips have not the power.

Ah! now those orbs grow eloquent!
    Yet eyes as bright I knew
In other moonlights long ago—
    That seemed to pierce me through,—

In moonlights radiant as this,
    When earth like Eden lay,
One made the night enchanted with
    A Flute he used to play.

Hark! . . there's the very strain he breathed,—
    A plaintive, melting air,—
'T is like a wounded heart's appeal,
    A lover's pleading prayer.

I wrote a tender ballad once,
    To give the theme a tongue:
A benediction and farewell--
    The saddest ever sung.

Like martial music now it peals!
    Anon, like sighing gales,
It winds a requiem for the brave
    Whose fate the Flute bewails.

I 've heard far finer harmonies,
    And played by master hands;
But naught that stirred me like that lay
    In other days and lands.

'But mother mine, the dark-eyed One,
    O who and where is he?'

I know not where. You touch the red
   Rose-heart of mystery.

'T was best we said Goodbye for aye,
   Though he was brave and true;
I have no woman's weak regrets.
   I 've much to love—and you.

Yet when that strain is played again
   In moonlights clear as this,
I feel a thrill steal o'er me still,—
   Words cannot all express.

Ah! now it comes adown the wind,
   It rises sweet and clear,
In liquid tones, that sink to moans,
   And die upon the ear.

Behind a cloud, as in a shroud,
   The moon pales in affright;
The hour grows wild—we 'll kiss, sweet child,—
   Speak low, and bid Good-night!

Expectation.

[Many years ago, my grandmother had a son who sailed for the West Indies. The ship put in for repairs at Cape Hatteras, left port, and was nevermore heard from. The fate of the young man remained a mystery, though, doubtless, he, with all on board, was engulfed in the sea. Yet long years after, my grandmother, with a mother's undying love, would look from her window for his possible return.]

A MOTHER sat by the window,
    With heart o'erburdened and sore,
While the purple tide came moaning in,
    And broke on the craggy shore.

In the silent, glimmering twilight
    The white-winged ships went by.
She tearfully mused on her darling boy,—
    O where did he linger, and why?

He had gone in his glorious manhood,
    With youth's unshadowed glee,
His mother's blessing on his ear,
    On the smiling, treacherous sea.

Wild music rang in the thicket,
    And pearls with roses were lain;
And the sky was aglow in the Long Ago,
    When he sailed on the shimmering main.

Ten laggard years went over,
    Yet came he nevermore;
But still she harks for his footfall sweet
    To ring on the old manse floor.

EXPECTATION.

O where is that noble brow lying,
  Those clustering curls of hair,
Those soulful eyes, and that manly form,—
  'Mid reefs of wet coral, is't there?

Was it for this she had borne him,
  Her heart's most affluent dower?
The fruit of fervid affection's past,
  Love bursting into flower?

What dreams her fancy had painted
  When the babe lay in cradled repose,
Of him as the sun of her happy life,
  And the evening star of its close!

Perhaps a mariner shipwrecked
  He lives on a foreign shore,
And by those fond maternal arms
  May be tenderly clasped once more.

Thus by the old manse window
  She keepeth love's vigil vain,—
For many a year may come and go,
  But he ne'er will return again.

We, too, are watchers expectant
  Upon life's seagirt beach.
Like apples of Tantalus, some sweet joys
  Will ever elude our reach.

Some plans of our life will be thwarted,
  Some ties that are dearest be riven,.
Till chastened we look for perfect bliss
  In Heaven—alone in Heaven!

Eyes of Blue.

I.

EYES of black or brown may sparkle,
    Laughing or with tender light,
Eloquent with mighty passion,
    Or mysterious as the Night—
    Wild and wildering as the Night.

II.

Brilliant hazel orbs entrance us,
    Hold us with a mystic spell.
All the heroes of romances
    With dark eyes their love-tales tell—
    Use their killing glances well.

III.

Black eyes oft, like darkened windows,
    Baffle when we look within;
Hide the thought in secret chambers,
    Lock the door and give no sign—
    Speak no tongue and soulless shine.

IV.

Eyes of gray belong to genius,
    Strong of purpose, clear of thought.
Piercing dark eyes, eyes that haunt us,
    May be fickle—trust them not.
    Ere they fool thee, spurn the spot.

V.
Blue eyes are the ones for feeling;
　　Blue eyes are the ones for truth.
Constant ever, roaming never,
　　Faithful to the dream of youth;
Welling o'er with generous ruth.

Angels of the Home.

[Written in loving remembrance of the noble men and women of our country who have given the writer entertainment and succor in her many years of lecture-work in the sacred cause of Temperance.]

I.

I HAVE seen them! I have seen them
　　Minister in many homes,
From the land of Pilgrim memories
　　To Francisco's stately domes.
Some were by the Eastern seaboard,
　　Some were in the land of Penn;
Hosts were in the cornclad prairies,
　　Many on the Western plain;
In the Rockies, in the plateaus,
　　In the stirring mining-camps;

Past where tall and snow-kissed mountains
  Glistened like electric lamps;
'Mid the groves of golden orange,—
  Where old Ocean laps the shore,—
Everywhere I found God's angels,
  And I bless them o'er and o'er.

II.

Everywhere they bade me welcome,
  Clasped my hand and drew me in;
Oft refreshed with royal bounty,
  Till my call was 'On!' again.
True, no aureole revealed them,
  Snowy pinions there were none.
They were pure and gentle women;
  They were stalwart, noble men!
But they guarded little children,
  Ministered at hearth and home,
Stayed up hands of Temperance herald,
  Sought to win the feet that roam;
And 'gainst Bacchus and Gambrinus
  Waged a just and holy war;
Leading in the thick of battle,
  Like brave Henry of Navarre!

III.

Clear I traced their highborn lineage,
  Children of the Heavenly King,
And I felt them household angels,
  Pluming then the snowy wing.
Oft, while up the crumbling stairway
  Of the years I've climbed since then,
Mem'ry's corridors were ringing

With their kindly steps again.
Oft their presence flits before me,
　With some generous deed or word,
And by tender recollections
　Deep my grateful soul is stirred:
And I pray the blessed Father,
　Who doth note the sparrow's fall,
To repay each noble action,
　And safe Home to guide them all.

IV.

O thou great and grand! my country!
　Ever be such homes thy own;
Multiply as stars of heaven,—
　Be thy firm foundation stone.
Homes of virtue, homes of freedom,—
　Where Love's sacred incense burns,
Where Religion builds her altar,
　Here the patriot hopeful turns.
For a people's best protection
　Is the hearth where true hearts dwell.
They are more than standing army,
　Arsenal or moated wall.
And where Church and Home and Schoolhouse
　Face the enemy's attack,
Let the haughty tyrant tremble!
　Let him send his minions back!

A Temperance Lyric.

Tune—"The moon is beaming o'er the lake."

I.

HARK! hark! what pealing anthems ring
   From mountain unto main?
Columbia's sons are marshaling
   To free the land again!
Refrain.—O comrades, shout the chorus out,
      Chorus rolling grand and free!
   O Temperance' starry flag stream out!
      Lead on to victory!
   At Temperance' call we're rallying all,
      United heart and hand,
   And this our battle-cry, "For God,
      And Home, and Native Land."

II.

Our cause is just, succeed we must,—
   Rum's legions soon will quail.
Their impious host will bite the dust,—
   Heaven will not let us fail.
Refrain.—O comrades, shout, etc.

III.

We'll rout base men from seats of power,
   We'll shield our homes from stain.
We'll guard what we have won in war,
   And all men's rights maintain.

O comrades, shout the chorus out,
　　Chorus rolling grand and free.
Oh, Temperance' starry flag stream out!
　　Lead on to victory!
At Temperance' call we are rallying all,
　　United heart and hand,
And this our battle-cry, "For God,
　　And Home and Native Land."

Refrain.

To the "Song of a Thousand Years."

RING out thy bells, my own Columbia!
　　Flash forth thy signal new unfurl'd,—
Glorious flag of Prohibition!
　　Banner of Freedom for all the world!

Which Way?

THE crisis is here and the issue is clear.
Will you vote for rum license and legalized ruin,
Or vote for your HOMES and vote as you PRAY?
Shall we barter the Boy for the gold of the dramshop?
No, never! I say. Home protection alway!
One ballot—just one—may win us the day!
So I solemnly ask, O Christian, O voter,
"Which way is your musket a-pointin' today?"

The Other Side.

I.

IT WAS quickly done! A low-voiced talk
To ears that drank undoubting in!
Henceforth with dimmer fame must walk
One who was pure within.

THE OTHER SIDE.

II.
'T was quickly done! A letter flew,
　　Bearing a soon-penned tale afar:
Unquestioned, were it false or true?
　　'T was poison in the air!

III.
On careless tongues the story grew.
　　Malignance helped to spread it wide.
Of all those whisperers scarce one *knew*
　　Or asked the Other Side!

IV.
The Other Side! Oh, had they known
　　The simple truth from first to last,
Mayhap their hearts had round her grown
　　And fondly held her fast!

V.
Misjudg'd, misunderstood; and so
　　Sharply misstated. This was all.
O gentle women! where the robes
　　Your charity lets fall?

VI.
Had ye but asked her, 'How is this?'
　　Told *her* the tale ye told elsewhere,
Ye would have seen she walked in white,
　　Ye would have found her heart sincere.

VII.
Unjust, if well-wrought work of years
　　Weigh naught against unchallenged breath.

And can suspicion's dart pursue
   An honest soul till death?

VIII.
Suspend your judgments. *Ye* may need
   That others wait ere they decide.
The grace you hope for, give. Take heed!
   There is Another Side.

Good Times.

WE dream of the By-and-by,
    When the children older be,
When our ships in the harbor lie,
    Now rocking in far-off sea;
When our schemings have well matured,
    When the new house we are in;
When fortune and fame are assured,—
    Then our GOOD TIMES will begin.

Today is hurry and toil;
    Scarce time for carol and prayer;
We labor by midnight oil,
    Till our brows are furrowed with care.
And sometimes the petulant word
    Or the quick retort of sin
Our nearest and loved have heard,
    And we fail their hearts to win.

We mean in the By-and-by,
    When our Good Times shall have come,
That Love shall illume the eye,
    And Wisdom direct our home.
We will give to the poor a token,
    We will visit and cheer the ill.
When, sudden, our thread is, broken!
    And the loom of our life is still!

Oh! alas! for the hearts not cherished!
  Alas, for the good not done!
Poor dreamers we were, who perished
  Ere the promised goal was won.
O trust to no doubtful future,
  Nor live so fast, I pray.
By kindness and meek forbearance
  Make *Good Times* of Today!

Oh, 't is not from wealth or leisure
  That good times chiefly come.
The sunny heart is a treasure,
  And maketh around it a home.
Defer not thy good till tomorrow;
  Exhale a sweet spirit today,—
No need from the future to borrow,—
  Thy Good Times shall be alway!

Almost Home.

CAN it be that tomorrow, or perhaps today,
 I shall cease from sorrow and pass away?
From the burning fever, from racking pain,
To wake o'er the River—to sweet rest again!

Have the sands in my hourglass to emptiness run?
Is the web of my life-work woven and done?
From doubting and fearing, from sighing and tears,
Can it be I am nearing the shadowless years?

From haste and from labor, from passion and strife,
How sweet to enter where love is life!
Where words are all tender, where hearts are all true,
Where the long rent asunder each fondly shall view!

I have known both summer and wintry days.
I do not murmur, but give God praise.
Not dark nor all dreary the way I have come,
Yet, Lord, I am weary. Am I almost home?

'Not yet, O my child.' (Sweet, sweet was the voice.)
'A mission is thine on the earth. Rejoice!
The crucible's heat was thy gold to refine.
Now gather me pearls from the deep-sea brine!

'Fear not. I will help thee. Each life is a plan.
Some day 't will appear how my love through it ran;
How tears turned to jewels: how tangles of gold
And scarlet were roses, when th' pattern's unrolled.'

The Flowers.

I.

THE Flowers! they are an alphabet
  Of Beauty writ by God;
In field and wood and valley set,
  And by the dusty road,
That lord and lady, rich and poor,
  And tawny rover wild
May read the lovely lesson o'er,
  With every little child.

II.

The Flowers are gracious thoughts from God
  To tender woman sent.
By couch of pain, 'neath coffin-lid,
  Their voice is eloquent.
They bid despairing hearts look up,
  To losses reconciled;
For He who tints the floweret's cup
  Cannot forsake His child.

III.

The Flowers are fairies on the lea.
  The violet is meek;
The lily white is purity;
  The rose hath love's own cheek.
The sunflower turns about her face,
  But ever seeks her god:

The purple asters bend with grace
  To greet the golden-rod.

IV.

The Flowers are subtle poetry,
  God writes upon the meads;
And he is wise who rev'rently
  The Master-poem reads.
The flowery balm is like the psalm
  Of holy, well-spent hours.
Oh, earth were robbed of wondrous grace
Were there no flowers, sweet flowers.

V.

When bird and bee go forth to woo
  Amid the fragrant dells,
The Flowerets offer cups of dew,
  They're such cold-water bell(e)s.
And when the sunset flag unfurls,
  And crimsons all the west,
The blossoms deck themselves with pearls,
  And are with glory drest.

Tokens of God.

IN Nature's face I love to look
And trace, as in an open book,
From starry orb to flower-gemmed sod,
The worthy tokens of a God.
Who formed for joy each living thing
That swims the sea, that soars on wing,—
Who paints the dawn, the sunset's gold,
Who formed for sight th' admiring eye,—
Who fills with life the field, the wold,
Who guides the birds that southward fly,—
Whose every work is perfect found,—
Who meted out creation's bound;
Who in their orbits holds the spheres;
Who bids the varying seasons move;
Whose harvest plenty crowns the years,—
Is surely Wisdom, Truth and Love!
His tenderest care for Man shall be
Man imaged like to Deity.
Believe,—His every law is still
A father's, not a despot's, will.
Obedience assures thy weal.
But who the ways of God refuse
Their own unhappiness do choose.
My King! Thou art so kind and good,
I mourn my willful, wayward mood.
O sheltering Ark! from seas of sin
Take a repenting wanderer in!

Mosses of Bright Memories.

I.

O THE moss, this beautiful moss!
Relic of land of the Chinee and Joss!
It grew in the vale by the sunset sea;
It festooned the boughs of a live-oak tree.
Pendulous,
    Swinging,
        Graceful it fell,
Like the filmy mesh of a lady's veil.
It brings back a rare and a radiant day,
When, after a sail o'er the smooth, bright Bay,
Through foothills to GEYSERS I took my way.
Oh, gay as a garden the long valley lay.

II.

Sweet springtime and beauty were weaving their spells.
What a blaze of wild flowers! what soft green in dells!
The live-oaks wore garlands of mosses as fair
As are wrought by the hand, with a lacemaker's care.
Springing,
    Galloping,
        Flying around
The mountain's steep edge, our steeds spurned the ground.
A failing bolt or a frightened leap
Had launched us over the awful steep.
    Our angels guarded from harm and loss.
Our guide drew rein by a moss-hung tree,

And a snap of his whip brought down to me
This curious, beautiful, treasured moss.

III.

Southward we turn, the Coast Range cross.
Observe this delicate Monterey moss.
Yonder sits Monterey, bride of the sea,
With the rime of the years where the cypress be.
Draping,
    Drooping,
        Clinging, the green
Of the fringing moss in low woods is seen.
Again on its wisp are memories strung,
Of the May when I roamed its old haunts among;
Of the picnic we held in the balm-dropping woods;
Of the voices that rang in the charmed solitudes,
Where, centuries gone, the Spaniard and Brave
Had heard, as I heard, the low-breaking wave.

IV.

Oh, this odorous, gold-green moss
    The giants of Mariposa wear;
Those ancient redwood kings that toss
    Their boughs three hundred feet in air.
Odorous,
    Emerald,
        Brilliant, see
A moss that has dwelt in high company.
Gathered from cedars that were not young
When Shakspeare played, when Dante sung;
    Anear Yosemite's wondrous vale.
What mighty secrets they could tell
Of changes which that coast befell;

Those monarchs o'er whose stately head
Eight solemn centuries have sped!

V.
Oh, this beautiful, trailing moss,
Pluckt where it thickly grew across
An ancient and ancestral grave,
Near where Atlantic's waters rave.
Creeping,
　　　Creeping,
　　　　　Night and Day,
Over the spot where my kindred lay.
My mother's mother! twine, sweet vine.
Noiseless trail, and creep, and twine
Over the dust where a sweet saint lies.
Guard till immortal it shall arise!
Live, like true love, that never dies!

To the Old Stone-Quarry.

[The crest of Ashton mentioned below is the highest point in Lee County, Illinois.]

I.

PLEASANT 't is on summer morning,
　　When dew-diamonds deck the spray,
Slumber's drowsy languor scorning,
　　O'er the hills to bound away;
Quaff from spring refreshing nectar,
　　Breathe large draughts of crystal air;
View the speaking face of Nature,
　　Night-refreshed, more charming fair.
Something of the outer beauty
　　Steals within the willing soul.
Something of the balm and gladness
　　Makes the wounded spirit whole.

II.

'T is my favorite, frequent fancy,
　　Ere the breakfast signals sound,
To the old, deserted quarry
　　O'er the hill to wind my round.
Up through avenues of maples,
　　Interlacing arms of shade,
Meeting on her milky errand,
　　Pail in hand, a star-eyed maid;
Up the emerald billow climbing,
　　Pause on Ashton's lofty crest.

Grand the prospect! Gaze far northward,—
Then look eastward, south and west.

III.

Lo! a vast and fertile valley;
    Fields on fields of heavy corn;
Mead and pasture, stream and woodland,
    Fattening herds of hoof and horn.
Miles on miles the landscape stretches,—
    Further still yon ridges blue.
Now look down. The Old Stone-Quarry's
    Excavation meets your view.
Deep,—deserted! miniature of
    Mighty valleys we have seen.
There unrolls the living Present,—
    Here's a grave of What Has Been!

Deeds.

'TIS wisdom's course the truth to *know*,—
    'T is wiser far the truth to *live*.
'T is kind to shed the tear for wo,—
    But still more kind, relief to give.

Like to Pygmalion's statue, cold
    And white and dead, are WORDS alone,—
DEEDS are as when the life-tides rolled,
    And maiden-love blushed in the stone.

Be Strong in Virtue and in God.

"The angel of the Lord encampeth round about them that fear Him, and delivereth them."—*Bible.*

OH, fear not, though invidious arts
    Be aimed against thee thick and fast;
Though Envy hurl her poisoned darts,—
    The battle will not always last.
The raging billows yet will cease;
The sea be hushed to perfect peace.

Strengthen thy spirit to endure.
    Then shall affliction's withered leaves
Enclose a rich, a lovely flower,
    And nature smile, while yet she grieves.
The soul, in meek submission bowed,
Beholds the rainbow in the cloud.

As buds, when crushed in fatal hour,
    Exhale their sweetest fragrance then,
So trials of the spirit's power
    Reveal its quenchless founts within.
And life's dark clouds, that o'er us fleet,
Make the successive light more sweet.

And deem not, if no answering tone
    From kindred souls responds to thee,
That no heart beateth like thine own,
    That no lute sounds in harmony.

This wide world may contain the strain
Responsive to thine own again.

Be strong in virtue. Ne'er depart
   From out that radiant zone of light.
Guard every action, word and thought,
   Pray God to keep thee in the right.
Then fearlessly and firmly move.
Thy course sublime Heaven will approve.

Moonlight in Winter.

HOW wondrous beautiful, 'neath Cynthia's light,
   The landscape, with its snowy veil, tonight!
In bridal vesture robed, Queen Earth appears,
Oblivious of her recent mood of tears.

On time-browned piles caressing moonbeams rove,
Like maiden's white arms round some wreck of love,
The wind is still, the scene's surpassing fair.
Tonight is Nature's coronation hour.

Oh, world of beauty! time of sweetest bliss!
Was ever moonlight beautiful as this?
Hours of poetic fancy, as ye roll
Impart some talisman unto my soul.

Listen, my heart; the benison is given;
It leads thy raptured thoughts to things in Heaven.
If so transcendant fair the world thou 'st trod,
How glorious, then, the Paradise of God!

Summer Moonlight.

MOONLIGHT over bright vales and flowers;
   Moonlight over the jasmine bowers;
Moonlight over the laborer's head
Moonlight over the slumbering dead.
Moonlight lay on the shining rill,
Wooed by the strain of the nightingale.
Moonlight shimmered amid the trees,
And danced with the leaflets in the breeze.
On diamonded grass and crystalline spring
Moonlight rested her gossamer wing;
Penciled with beauty each turret brown,
And hung her white flag over village and town.
Her silvery sheen in magnificence lay
Where light waves of ocean were leaping at play,
And myriad lamps shone brilliantly there,
For every bright billow reflected a star!

SUMMER MOONLIGHT.

Moonlight unfurled her luminous tent
In the azure court of the firmament;
And her radiant zone, with its gems of light,
Was a jeweled crown on the brow of night.
So beauteous the scene, so witching its power,
It almost seemed, in that mystical hour,
That the windows of Heaven were open thrown,
And a glimpse of its glory to mortals was shown.
The maiden mild and the convict of crime
Felt each the spell of that hallowed time.

Oh, if there be moments when Mercy and Peace
    With balm-dropping sandals e'er tread the green earth,
Bidding the clamors of Passion to cease
    And saintly affections to spring to their birth,
When guardian angels are hovering round us,
Sundering fetters that downward have bound us;
When the Right should exert its holiest power,—
'T is in sweet summer-time, at the moonlight hour.

God's Way.

IT IS said that when the mother-bird
  Would teach her young to use its wings,
She bears it, perched upon her back,
  Beyond the nest, and from it springs.
The startled birdling flutters down,
  Like windblown leaf, unto the ground.
But soon, with pinions stronger grown,
  Its glorious power to soar has found.

So, Lord, from out the well-loved nest,
  Thy providence hath borne Thy child,
And dropped her where it pleased Thee best,
  Though weak of heart, scarce reconciled.
And she hath found, once and again,
  That thus Thou ledst to larger things.
The wider vision,—fuller strain,—
  More heavenward flight of spirit wings.

Invocation of Water.

I.

HAIL, crystal Water!
    Bright, bright and free.
Ho! son and daughter,
    Here's the draught for thee.
Bubbling in the fountain,
    Singing through the lea;
Laughing in the mountain,
    Booming in the sea!
Hail, sparkling Water!
    Clear, bright and free,—
Ho! son and daughter,
    Here's health for thee.

II.

Hail, blessed Water!
    Type of Purity.
Quaff, son and daughter,
    From the fountain free.
Now it glows a rainbow,
    In the magic sun;
Now it sleeps in rose-heart,
    When the day is done.
Hail, blessed Water!
    Lave the debauchee,—
Smiling son and daughter,
    Here's wealth for thee.

III.

Pledge with crystal Water!
    Speed the jubilee,
When each son and daughter
    From rum's curse is free.
Leave the brimming beaker!
    Serpents ambush there!
Leave the winecup's revel,-
    'T is madness and despair!
Hail, crystal Water!
    Bright, bright and free.
Ho! son and daughter,
    Here's the glass for thee!

A Test.

IF Penitence and Charity
    Be strangers to thy heart,
Though fair thy outer life may be,
Think not the gates of pearl for thee
    Will promptly spring apart.

With deep distress the Publican
    Confessed and was forgiven.
The Pharisee was free from stain,
But, haughty to a brother-man,
    Was not approved of Heaven.

Old Age.

A PLEASANT fire and an easy chair,
    Set where the light falls clearly,—
Plain, nourishing food, with converse good,
And a soft, clean bed for the limbs and head,—
    These make Old Age go cheerly.

A treasured book for the sunny nook,
    Anon the friendly letter;
The outdoor walk, the genial talk,
The kindly deed to a soul in need,
    These make Old Age completer.

But Age must give as well as take,
    Must bear some ills serenely;
Must wear no frown, nor seek its own,
But hope and love, unfailing on,
    Till crowned in Heaven, queenly.

The Village Bell.

SWEETLY peals from its ivied tower
Yon deep-toned Bell, at the vesper hour.
Lingering echoes seem to say,
Thoughtless spirit, haste and pray!
Come, where voices in praise are blending;
Come, thy knee in penitence bending.
Life is flying and death is near.
Wayworn traveler, worship here.

Many a year that bell has swung,
And a thing of life is its tireless tongue
Now it thrills with a tender mood,
Anon it thunders over the wood.
It calls to school and the swarming street,
Rings with a troop of pattering feet.
When furious flames are towering high,
It sounds the tocsin, and men fly!

A sacred thing is that old church bell.
'T is freedom's herald and slavery's knell.
When the baleful star of rebellion arose,
And brothers to brothers grew deadliest foes,—
When the groans of defeat men trembled to hear,
Its peans of triumph rang grandly and clear,
And deepened and swelled when tyranny's chain
Was struck from the necks of three millions of men!

A vision comes of a well-known time,
When the church bell rang with a wedding chime.

THE VILLAGE BELL.

Sweet flowers breathed on the ambient air,
And the fairest Flower of all was there.
There flashed a glimmer of satin and lace,
As the bridal cortege took its place.
The vow was breathed and the twain made one,
And life looked bright as the hues of the sun.

A five-month passed, and the village bell
Mournfully tolled a funeral knell.
O joy and grief, ye were quickly allied.
'Neath that sable pall was the saintly bride!
A weeping train laid her tenderly down
To her dreamless rest, while the bell tolled on.
And I think, as it vibrates so solemn and slow,
Some day they will toll it, and lay me low.

Old Father Time.

THE year rolls by. How ceaselessly
  Old Father Time speeds on!
In heat, in cold, by day, by night,
  His march is never done.

When weeping eyes are closed in sleep,
  And hearts forget their care,
Old Time ascends some distant steep,
  Or treads in fields of air.

From whence he came, or where he goes,
  No mortal eye hath seen.
No wavelet of the trackless air
  Reveals where he has been.

No rustle of mysterious wings
  Betrays his rapid flight.
But naught can check his course sublime,
  Through regions veiled from sight.

No storm-cloud with o'ershadowing pall,
  No light of roseate sky,
No joy, nor grief, nor prayers detain
  Yon traveler rushing by.

There comes a deep, mysterious roar,
  As of a mighty sea,

That tells us Time is near the shore
    Of vast Eternity,

Where each must launch a little barque
    And sail through endless years,
Poor children wildered in the dark,
    Beleagured with our fears.

Yet all we've felt of human love,
    Or learned of the divine,
Assures, beyond God's pitying care,
    We cannot cross the line.

Only the unrepenting still
    No port of peace shall win;
Self-doomed to hell, the stubborn will
    That still prefers to sin.

Oh, Traveler Time! whose flight sublime
    Was from creation's birth,
Teach me true wisdom, as I climb
    With thee the steeps of earth.

What is Love?

I.
SINCE first the stream of Time began,
    When earth was young,
When to sweet Eve the primal man
    His love-tale sung,
In every age, in every zone,
The blind and prankish god has thrown
    His darts the swains among.
And countless Psyches have confessed
The pleasure-pain that thrilled their breast.

II.
It comes, the bright, all-conquering flame,
    To high, to low,
To shepherd lad, to titled name,
    Hot blood, and slow.
No armor doth 'gainst Love prevail.
More eloquent the one old tale
    Than dulcet Music's flow.
Its power the hardest heart can move.
Yet many differ, WHAT IS LOVE?

III.
Is it the spell which beauty weaves
    O'er lover's eye?
A fever in young blood, that leaves
    When time steals by?

The magnetism of man and maid?
Will 't end when Hymen's vows are said,
   Demanding liberty?
Is 't born of kisses, finger-tips,—
Forgot at parting from the lips?

IV.

Is it a mystery quite apart
   From Reason's sphere?
Have noble virtues of the heart
   Small influence here?
Are pure devotion, sentiment,
Frail shadows from Love's substance sent,
   Not its best cheer?
Are souls by true affection moved,
Whose fondest dream 's but to be loved?

V.

Nay! Heaven-born love seeks others' bliss,
   Not self-attent.
It grows sublime with sacrifice,
   A sacrament.
'T will *give* its all, as well as take—
Counts labor sweet for dear ones' sake,
   Its largess free, unspent.
Once loved, upon life's highest plane,
Is *loved forever* without wane.

Found at an Inn.

TWINKLED and glowed on the murky air
    The great red eye of the inn;
And while we mused by the evening fire,
    Our host a scroll brought in.
Whether 't was dropped by a lady fair,
    Or a sad, regretful man,
No clue was there to the secret rare,
    But thus the stanzas ran:

THE SCROLL.

I.

This letter is written from home, Hal,—
    I have been long away.
The shadows at last are lengthening fast,
    With me it is not May.
I have returned to the dear old friends,
    And the old-time haunts as well,
The campus, the chapel, and once have heard
    The peal of its musical bell.

II.

O memories! how ye come surging up,
    As wave on wave of the sea!
I think of the glorious future we dreamed,
    And muse on the beings we be!
Back, back to your cells, nor fashion your spells
    Over my fancy again!

FOUND AT AN INN.

Can ye unwrite the tale of a life,
And make me a glad girl again?

III.

This morning the heavens were azure, Hal,
  The bluebirds sang on the bough.
All golden the air, and nature as fair
  As twenty long summers ago.
My course I took over willowy brook
  Along the white-clover blooms,
Through pastures green that lay between
  My home and the old college rooms.

IV.

Sure you will remember the footpath, Hal,
  That led from the house on the hill,
Through thicket with sumac and maple aflame,
  Where the plaint of the turtle-dove fell.
O'er billowy fields whose broad crown yields
  To a brook in a valley of shade,
Along whose brim, as a Bluebeard grim,
  A hoarse-throated watchdog bayed!

V.

Near a little brown house the foot-trail ran.
  There often, 'neath sunset skies,
A maiden passed on; and a deep-voiced man
  Followed the girl with his eyes.
They met each day in the old college hall;
  They studied the same old books,
And the tender inflections of *amo* grew
  From words to tenderer looks.

VI.

It all came back to my memory, Hal,
  Though twenty long summers ago.
The world without and the world within
  Have altered somewhat, I trow.
The tangled thicket's a well-trimmed grove,
  The field is a fairground now;
The tiny green path is a deep-cut road,
  Where rumbling horsecars go.

VII.

The little brown house is still on the slope,
  But the charm of the meadow is gone.
The soon-parted twain met scarcely again;
  Their youth and its poem are flown.
You toy with the curls of your baby boy, Hal,
  The maid you remember no more,—
And she can glance at a dead romance,
  Smile softly, and say, 'It is o'er!'

Parting.

FRIEND, fare thee well! stern Fate doth sever
True hearts that could live in smiles forever.
With pitiless grasp he wrenches in twain
The glittering clasps of affection's chain.
He scattereth blossoms from Love's bright tree.
He severeth friends with changeless decree.

Drops from one source may dissevered become.
In lines diverging their channels may run.
And when, O when, will they mingle in one?
They meet in the ocean. 'T is thus with our life.
We're parted by earth's commotion and strife.
But oh, may Love's compass from Jesus be given,
To guide o'er the foam-capped billows to Heaven,
And there in a happier clime may we dwell.
Till then, dear heart, fare thee well! farewell!

Four Voices of Life.

[For parlor or Sunday-school entertainments. To be impersonated with full tableau in conclusion. Has been successfully used in Chicago.]

I. CHILDHOOD.

MOSS-ROSE! Red-rose! White-rose so fair,
Give me your sweet buds to bind in my hair.
Buttercup! Buttercup! lend me thy gold.
Rainbow! Rainbow! I would thee enfold.
    I'll speed like the wind
      Thy pillars to find,
        And thy gold pots to hold.
White Cloud! Snow Cloud! what hast thou done
With thy banners of crimson aflaunt in the sun?
Hast sailed with the angels that float in the air? –
And where is Heaven? Pray, tell me where.

II. YOUNG MAIDENHOOD.

Childhood is o'er,—a fast fading shore,
Its joys and its pastimes can hold me no more.
I have dreampt of Fame, but Fame is strife.
I have longed for Wealth, but Love is Life!
    This hour I wait
    For my hero, my fate—
    And alas! he is late.
Come life, come death, I will love him more
Than ever maiden oved man before!
Come hither to me, by the old elm-tree;
The stars are watching and winking for thee!

While thou dost delay, the moon sinks low—
The red rose faints that was pluckt for thee now—
The nightingale stops her song on the bough.
O hark! by that sign he is coming, I know.
Yet hide thy joy, O heart of mine.
Too quickly won—may quickly pine;
And he must be true, my Man of men!

III. MATERNITY.

My pretty one, my precious joy!
Blessings upon thee, cherub boy.
Thy father sails the trackless sea,
And toils afar for thee and me.
Oh, when to riper stature grown,
Say, wilt thou in the ships be gone?
Nay! nay! in manhood's proud estate,
At home thou shalt be wise and great;
This dimpled hand work well its part;
    This voice be music in my ear;
This eye subdue some girlish heart,
    And beam upon thy nestlings dear.
Sleeps! sleeps! my baby sleeps,—
And Love its sacred vigil keeps,
My dove so mild, my undefiled!
A woman's crown is her sinless child.

IV. A GOLDEN OLD AGE.

All is ended, the joy and the sorrow.
No fire of life's passions can kindle my morrow.
All that were dearest are parted from me,
One in the churchyard and one in the sea.
Yet often their spirits seem round me still.
We shall meet some day in God's sweet will.

All I've to live for is serving my race.
All men are my brothers; a sister I trace
In the face of each woman, whatever she be.
The heart that has suffered is nearest to me.
Here's a hand for the fallen! for sorrow a tear.
Here's a smile for the happy! for all I've a prayer.
The One who never can fail us, I know,
Was smitten with grief and acquainted with wo.
To Him, O my sisters, O friends, let us go.

Thus living and loving, from out of earth's fire,
To the home of the soul I aspire! I aspire!

"Grumble Alley and Thankful Street."

COME out of "Grumble Alley," come into "Thankful Street."
Stay not in darksome valley, where Gloom and Anger meet.
Sit not stone-blind to Beauty, brooding thy grief and hate,
But mount the hills of Duty, and nobly meet thy fate.

Dost bend with burdens double? True grace will help thee bear.
Dost dread impending trouble? Perhaps 't will melt in air.
Bemoanst thy small resource? Think, some beside their dead
Would part with golden purse to bring back sunny head.

Bewailst thy single talent? Safe thou from Envy's stings;
From jarring dissonance of harp of thousand strings.
Is thy good work unmarked? thou slighted and passed by?
Just recompense is sure. One noted from on high.

Look out. The world is bright; the birds sweet strains
    prolong.
Turn from thy bosom's night, and join great Nature's song.
Oh, tossed and full-of-cares! a good God reigns o'er all.
Trust Him who counts thy hairs and marks the sparrow's
    fall.

Take up thy nearest duty, with stout and hopeful heart.
Speak words of love and beauty. Do well thy lowly part.
Heroic patience rally and Peace thy soul will greet,
And lead from Grumble Alley to cheery Thankful Street.

If, from the fields Elysian, we saw our earthly lot;
That clearer, juster vision would still oft-fretting thought.
Since "all things work together" to make for glory meet.
Then welcome, stormy weather! All's well in Thankful
    Street.

The Chance Meeting.

WE met in youth's bright springtime
    Its blossoms in our hands;
Its sunshine in our laughing eyes,
    Its mirage o'er our lands.

We ranged the field of letters;
    We gathered fancy's flowers.
We found a mutual sympathy
    That charmed the passing hours.

Such dainty missives came and went
    As rhyme or reason sends.
We glanced at deeper sentiment,
    And then we parted—friends.

We drifted long and far apart.
    A score of years went o'er.
And who was wed, or who was dead,
    We knew and thought no more.

Till lately down this strange, great town
    I went my stormy round.
The frost-wind cut like steel without,
    The snow lay on the ground.

I sat beside an office fire.
    A gentleman was there.

Long-bearded, portly, . . . an M. D.?
Professor, . . . by his air.

We passed some commonplace remark;
He went his distant way,
And neither guessed what friends had met,
And parted, too, that day!

The Dreamer.

I.

AH! you picture an artist's studio,—
Hair raven, eyes like the night,—
You think of Phidias, Raphael, Angelo,
With masterful hand and thought-heavy brow.
Ah, no-
You read not my riddle aright.

II.

What then? some glorious scholar
Toiling in midnight cell?
A Radical leaving ancestral halls,
Splendors and titles and sculptured walls?
'T were well.
But simpler the story I tell.

III.

Not even a maiden's pure chamber,
    Snowily, vestally white;
With incense of flowers borne in on the breeze,
With rapture of bird-song flung in from the trees,—
        Beautiful, bright;
    Our sketch hangs in different light.

IV.

Only a homely brown building,
    Set deep in the heart of the town;
Twelve girls at work; and the master's eye,
Urging the business silently,
        On, ever on,
    Till darkness her curtain lets down.

V.

Work, work, from the dewy morning,
    And work till daylight is o'er.
But youth is elastic, and girls are gay,
And labor is mingled with chatter and play,
        The livelong day,
    With "Bleachery" over the door.

VI.

Their words, while their fingers are flying,
    Are the froth of the o'erfoaming glass:
The moment's fancy; the tint of a rose;
The droop of your hat; the style of their beaux;
        Alas! alas!
    For the free, careless talk of a lass!

VII.

Why sitteth fair Rosabel silent,
    With look of some far-away sphere?
Nor joins in the ripple of laughter sweet,
Nor heeds the passer-by over the street?
        Not here, I fear,
    Is her heart, though her service is here.

VIII.

For Love, the wonderful charmer,
    Has touched the maid with his wand;
And she dwells in a land of enchantment now,
And her sky is lit with a beautiful glow,—
        A glamour I know,—
    And his zephyrs her senses have fanned.

IX.

Oh, the wondrous illusions of Love!
    Oh, the whitest day that is o'er!
The miracle by all ages approved,
When first we believe *we love and are loved!*
        Earth hath no more
    Transcendent bliss to add to our store!

X.

So Rosabel dreams of her lover,
    The hero so brave to her view;
Of tenderest husband and faithfullest wife,
Ennobling and blessing a mutual life.
        My friend, think you
    Her visions will ever come true?

XI.

O Destiny, what of this Dreamer?
  Whisper it softly and slow.
The twain that love fondly will soon be divided,
And each to another be solemnly wedded.
    Soon, dreamless and low,
  The maiden will sleep where the myrtles blow.'

Her Postscript.

I.

I KNOW my words are simple,
  But I love you night and day;
And whether comes storm or sunshine,
  I'll love you ever, I say.

II.

I never tire repeating
  These words so sweet to me.
Oh! could they utter the ardor,
  The depth of my feeling to thee!

III.

'T is said Love's chains are silken.
  They are not chains to me;

But as a glad bird seeks her mate,
    So flies my heart to thee.

IV.

My name, that seemed so homely,
    You breathed—'t is prettier grown,
And yours I think the sweetest
    That I have ever known.

V.

Yes, I will wait for you, dearest,
    Through years of good or ill;
This thought will make them half divine—
    We love each other still!

Interrogation.

I.

HAS change crept o'er thy spirit yet?
    In one brief hour is love forgot?
I wait for thee—at noon—at night—
    Till hope expires—thou comest not!
If thou dost love, how canst thou live
    So near and yet so long apart?
Nor send one word or sign to flash

Electric heat from heart to heart?
Are not our souls attuned as one?
Then is my pain *my* pain alone?

II.

I've scorned to doubt. I've held such thoughts
  Disloyal, and I bade them go.
And yet, were I a man like thee,
  I could not treat my true love so.
Thou badst me read thy troth sincere,
  In all thy acts. The proof is blurred;
The explanation's locked from me;
  Thou hast the key. I wait thy word.
But, O my king! if thou shouldst be
Unkind or false, 't were death to me.

III.

Too late, when fondest hearts are fled,
  Deep sighs to breathe, sad tears to shed.
When Paradise, we prized too late,
  Is barred, and angels guard the gate.
Then hasten, dear, fly straight to me!
  While ghostly terrors of the night
Fold up their tents and trooping flee,
  Fill thou my life with love and light.
If thy dear love be all my own,
Come, and our bliss will be begun!

Estranged.

DEAD!—yet not dead!—ah me,
    That it is so!
'T was all so different
    One year ago,
Oft I recall the blissful hour,
When life burst forth in perfect flower!
There beamed new brightness in the air,
There streamed enchantment everywhere.
December seemed as gay as June,
The runnels purled a merry tune,
The founts of joy did so o'erflow,
My very heart did bud and blow!
To music danced the feet of Time,
For One was near, and One was mine!
And I was brave, whate'er befall,
For One was near, and One was all!
    Ah me!
What ecstasy, lost Love, with thee!
Methought I never lived before.
Alas! 't is death, if love be o'er.
What pure communion, just control,
Marked the discourse of soul with soul!
Yet what endearing words were said,
While each for each a heaven made!
All other joys sank in eclipse

At final meeting of the lips!

Today it seems so long ago . . .
    So many tears since then I've shed,
My heart's so heavy now, I know
    'T is *I* am dead!

Sing to Me Now of Jesus.

'SING us a song, my daughter,'
    A tremulous old man said.
'T was the still hour, made for music,—
    The sun had sunk to his bed.
And all in the pensive gloaming
    The darkness deepening fell,
And naught was heard save one lone bird,
    With his plaint of Whip-poor-Will.

Then in the large old farmhouse,
    To the organ's solemn chords,
The maiden sang, and the night-air rang
    To the theme of tender words.
Perhaps 't was Annie Laurie,
    Or the Emigrant's Lament,

And "It may be for years and it may be forever,"
Whose charm with the sweet hour blent.

Intently the aged one listened
  To the strains that rose and fell,
To the dreamful voice of his daughter dear,
  And he felt the musical spell.
"Those songs are sweet," he murmured,
  "But I seem to miss one name.
Oh, sing to me now of Jesus;
  I am longing to hear of Him."

He was nearing the swelling river,
  Which each must cross alone.
He was nearing the Realm of Spirits,
  The world unseen, unknown;
Nearing the awful secrets
  Beyond the night so drear,
He wanted fast hold of Jesus,—
  He longed for the heavenly cheer.

Then the old hymns, sweet and holy,
  She sang till he went to rest,
And the peace of God on his soul was shed,
  And soothed the troubled breast.
Oh! hymns we heard in childhood,
  Beside our mother's knee,—
Repeat them gently when we shall stand
  On the verge of the solemn sea.

Shipwreck.

I.
CALM was the eve, and wondrous bright,
  O'er silver lake and town.
Queen Dian rode a car of light,
  And dropped her smiling glances down,
    O'er slumbering Michigan,
      A silent glory white.

II.
Oh, who could guess from night so fair
  The rising, deadly gale?
The carnival of sprites in air,
  The cruel surge, the flapping sail,
    The cheek with terror pale,
      The faltered, gasping prayer?

III.
On shore they slept, undreaming bale;
  Some to embark at morn.
But ere day broke, began to wail
  Uncanny winds, with sounds forlorn,—
    To whisper, shriek and moan,
      With weird and ghostly tale.

IV.
At dawn the Fiends are mustering,—
  Wild clouds shut in the sky;

SHIPWRECK.

Big raindrops fall with startling ring,—
The marshal'd winds like furies fly,—
Waves lift their hands on high,—
The Storm, the Storm is King!

V

Now fiercer rage the powers of air,
The vast lake heaves and boils.
Wo! for the luckless boat caught there,
Where brave Alpena frantic toils
Deep! thou wilt have fresh spoils,
Nor for their anguish spare.

VI.

The flashing whitecaps mount the skies,
The engulfing channels yawn
She sinks, doomed ship —no more to rise,
Her host to watery grave have gone.
Moan! moan! blast sweeping on,
With deep and mighty cries.

VII.

Three days the hurricane prevailed,
Lashing the lake and shore.
Whatever craft the waters sailed
Was wrecked or madly driven o'er.
Such awful gale before
To find the oldest memory failed.

VIII.

With thunderous roar, winds grappled rock;
On shore smote giant trees.
They fell like pipe-stems at the shock,
Or troops mown down by batteries.

The wreck-strewn forest lies
Like towns where earthquakes rock.

IX.

At length the elemental burst,
    Resistless, gloomy, bold,
Had spent its force and wrought its worst.
    But oft in vision wives behold
Those billows mountain-high—
    Spray blinding rock and sky.

Unloved.

Oh, give me love, true love alone
    My yearning spirit cries.
Silent I wait for an answering tone,
    For tender and sweet replies.

In vain. There's dew for the thirsty ground,
    Sunshine for the buds unblown;
Each wild bird its mate hath found.
    Only my heart is lone.

Yet have I dreampt of a manly form,
    And a spirit strong and true;
And a sunny nook unreached by storm,
    Where sweetest home-joys grew.

I've seen, alas! those hopes decay,
    And yet for love I sigh;
Chasing as desert-travelers may
    The mirage in the sky.

For wealth or fame can never still
    An aching heart's unrest,
Nor void in woman's nature fill;
    Unloved, she is unblest.

Then give me love; for it I pine
    As the captive in his cell;
As the bird encaged for the soaring range
    Of the woods he loved so well.

Only an echo-sound replies,
    And the whispering air is still!
The half-born hope within me dies,
    And the night grows dark and chill.

Still for affection's sacred boon
    My anguished prayer will rise,
Will it ne'er wake an answering tone,
    With tender and sweet replies?

The Monody of Dolorosa.

I.
'I AM alone—worn and alone,'
   To herself she said;
'No tender voice when day is done,
No soft caress of a loving one,
   Though I am wed.

II.
'These tasteful rooms I dress with care
   For whom, aye, whom?
For smiles that bless me on the stair?
For a heart that holds me ever fair?
   Alas! my doom.

III.
'I've been a wife full many a year,
   Helpful and true;
Sure all his griefs and burden to share.
Are food, a roof and something to wear
   A wife's full due?

IV.
'Can creature-comforts gauge the reach
   Of the spirit's wants?
The converse sweet, the softened speech—
The flow of heart from each to each—
   For these it pants.

THE MONODY OF DOLOROSA.

V.
'The sympathy of kindred souls,
    The ways of Love . . .
The generous preference that controls,
The clasp that saith, while it enfolds,
    Rest here, my dove!

VI.
'He will not . . . perhaps cannot . . . speak
    What lovers frame.
He deems me foolish, willful, weak.
His words are blows that rudely break
    My life's fond dream.

VII.
'I stifle in these prison walls
    As in a tomb.
No childhood patters through these halls,
Nor baby prattle softly falls
    To break the gloom.

VIII.
'Great God! are hearts so little worth
    Grown wild with pain,
That men may tread them in the earth,
And then walk confidently forth,
    And wear no stain?

IX.
'Oh, would he say 'Forgive, forgive,'
    My love would live!'
And then her voice sank to a moan;
'But no! I feel I must go on
    Alone! alone!'

Jack and Polly.

I.

SOMETIMES the young indulge in scorning
The older people's sober warning,
That he who "drinks" gets soft and mellow,
And yield an ear
To what they hear
From some gay, plausible *young* fellow.
My lads, 't is wise
To take your seniors' good advice.

II.

Jack was a confident gallant,
Who, after day's work, often went
Some miles to woo a farmer's daughter.
Their homes between
A pool was seen—
A long, wide marsh of muddy water.
Jack, starting early,
Walked round the pond to see Miss Polly.

III.

One night, attired in all his best,
White linen suit and gorgeous vest,
He reached the hollow marsh belated.
'T was miles around.
Now, why not bound
Across, and soon to Poll be mated?

"Waist-deep! waist-deep!"
The old frogs croak, the old frogs peep.

IV.
"Waist deep? O pshaw!" Jack quickly said.
"I better know with half a head.
'T is shallow; one could wade across 't.
I 'll well prepare,
And soon be there,
And gain the full hour I have lost."
"Knee-deep! knee-deep!
'T is but knee-deep!" the *young* frogs peep.

V.
Jack took the *younger* frogs' advice,
Rolled up his garments in a trice,
And, wading in, soon learned his folly.
The waters rose—
Waist-deep he goes!
Oh, he has spoiled his fine white clothes!
He was a sight to laughing Polly.
Ashamed and cold,
His love untold,
He homeward sneaked, no longer bold;
And at the pool
The frogs all screamed, "Old fool!
Old fool! old fool!"

Vesper Memories.

DAY'S crimson flush has faded.
    The silence broodeth all.
The lovely earth is shaded
    By night's o'erhanging pall.

Star after star is beaming,—
    I heed no more their ray.
I dreaming, fondly dreaming,
    My heart is far away.

I think of words thou'st spoken,
    Words spoken once to me.
Oh, with a love unbroken,
    I think of thee—of thee!

A Lover's Remonstrance to His Dear.

I.

LAST month your letters blossomed out
    In words the Love-God sends;
But yesternight there fell a blight,—
    'Hereafter write as friends.'

II.

I conned it o'er, amazed and sore.
    The arrow pierced my heart.
By silence pride the wound would hide,
    But deep remained the smart.

III.

For I have loved you truly, sweet,
    And hung on 'Yours till death.'
You seemed the soul of constancy.
    Oh, was it only breath?

IV.

I yield henceforth to your decree,
    Will write but friendly letters.
I give you back your fealty.
    I hold you by no fetters.

V.

If on another you can smile,—
    Allow some happier man

To wear the heart I held awhile,
I'll bear as best I can.

VI.

I would not on your happiness
A grief or shadow cast.
You filled my heart with heavenly bliss.
Alas! it did not last.

VII.

Oh, wherefore is the limit set?
If I have erred, reveal.
I cannot yet your troth forget;
I have some tokens still.

VIII.

And I will strive so pure to live,—
So grandly, squarely do,
You'll write, though late,—'Behold, I wait
For you, love, only you!'

A Daydream Ended.

THE dream of the heart, it hath fled as the shade
That moves like a phantom o'er mountain and glade.
Yet even the shadows so airy and gray
Have a rare grace exceeding the beauty of day.

Return, dear Dream! come back to me yet.
Thy wondrous enchantment I cannot forget.
The visits of angels methinks could not be
So charmed and divine as thy visions to me.

No more—ah, no more! too wild was the blast.
The Dream of the years is entombed with the past.
My long-cherished hopes a moment must quiver,
Like a lute's broken strings, then be voiceless forever!

Though stars have been beaming with silvery light,
Yet tears are now dimming those eyes of the night;
And clouds, with their gloomy and desolate frown,
Like high tides of ocean now swiftly come on.

The fond heart still flutters, a bird in the rain,
Vainly beating its wings 'gainst the flame-lighted pane.
It must hence from the vision of comfort and cheer,
And enter the tempest. Its rest is not here.

Yet, Love, hadst thou perished, but tender and true,
I had loved thee forever, had loved only you.

Thy mem'ry I'd cherished still green in my heart,
And felt thou wert still of my being a part.

But wo to the soul whose idol was clay, -
Alone o'er its wreck to wrestle and pray.
The halo is flown, the false prop is gone,—
The world spins around, and it sinks in a swoon!

Mosaic-Workers.

I.

SOME built with massive piles of stone
   The Pyramids, the Pantheon,
     Through centuries to endure,—
The glory of the ages gray,
The marvel of our world today,
     Of fadeless fame secure.
And some with colored bits, and small,
Built tessellated, pictured wall,
     And rare Mosaic floor.
Alone, each fragment worthless seemed;
Combined, the work with genius gleamed;
And flower and star and order grew
Beneath their workmanship so true.
     Alike the great, the small
     Have made the Art-world beautiful.

II.

Among the poets of all time
A royal few wrought verse sublime.
 Like giant trees they stand,
That nigh a thousand years ago
In Mariposan groves did grow,—
 Or like cathedrals grand.
Did they exhaust the epic themes?
Our age not unheroic seems,
 Whose sons for Native Land,
And God, and Home and Liberty
Went forth to bravely do or die!
Many, Mosaic-Workers be,
Weaving their ballads skillfully.
 They, too, with patient toil,
Create the Fair, the Beautiful.

III.

Our lives are all Mosaics rare,
No two alike, each planned with care
 By Artist infinite.
Some rosy pink, some gold and white,
Some gray, and some like solemn night,
 Each fitted bit to bit.
The pattern oft we fail to see,
And careless mar the symmetry,
 And dull the marbles white.
We are as children larger grown;
We spoil the plan, we break the stone,
And o'er the wreck we moan and cry.
But pity fills our Father's eye;
And when we all to Him resign,
He makes the dimmed Mosaics shine!

A Dream of Arcady.

I.

A MAN of cares, no longer young,
    I dwell amid the busy town.
My clerks may note, with gallant tongue,
    The willowy form, the silken gown;
May walk the dreamy lanes of love,
    And drain the brimming cup of joy.
Far otherwise my destinies move,
    Far other themes my thoughts employ!
As men, when banished Eden see,
I view my lost, fair Arcady!

II.

Yet I have known Love's alphabet,—
    The smile, the blush, the sigh, the tear;
The ecstasy of love returned.
    'T is o'er, alas! and I am here.
But sometimes, bending o'er my book,
    I see instead a wistful face,
In whose true eyes I used to look
    And all its tender heaven to trace!
And for a moment comes to me
A blissful glimpse of Arcady.

III.

Last eve, when riding up the street,
    I saw a modest, youthful pair—

A manly youth, a lassie sweet.
   I smiled, but envied. Love was there!
What was a costly boarding-place
   To welcomes . . such as I had known?
The fond exclaim, the arms' embrace,
   The eyes that told a heart my own!
The constant soul; true sympathy;
   While each for each made Arcady!

IV.

Home altars have been wrecked by change,
   And incompatibility.
I 'll ne'er believe I would have tired
   Of her, or she of me.
Forever shrined in one true heart,
   Undimming, her ideal lives.
We would have walked in naught apart,—
   She proved the model of all wives.
Whate'er betide, our barque should glide
   O'er silver tide in Arcady!

V.

Come back the music of thy voice!
   Come back the days when by my side!
Come back, the heaven of our joys,
   In God's good time, come, and abide!
Yet, mayhap, better prayer would be,
   (Her memory sacred in my breast,)—
Lord, I refer it back to Thee;
   Whate'er Thou dost, it is the best.
But let Thy love around her be,
Whom once I knew in Arcady.

The Sundown Sea.

I.

OH, the Sunset Sea! Oh, beautiful Sea!
Mighty, limitless, vast and free!
I stand on the shore of the golden lands,
Where the white curling waves lap silvery sands,
And list to the measured shock and speech
Of billows that break on the sounding beach.
And, gazing as far as the sight can go,
See the liquid stretch and the ceaseless flow.
And never the shimmer and gray glimmer dies
Till the blue of the sea meets the blue of the skies.

II.

Oh, the Sundown Sea, ever bounding and free!
Unfettered and bold in thy grand majesty!
Yon good ship rides on thy heaving breast
To the spicy green isles of the purpling West.
Ah! many have stood by the smiling Bay,
And seen their argosies sailing away;
And waited and watched at the Golden Gate,
For their ship that was due—their ship that was late.
Oh, wonderful, trackless, treacherous Sea!
Deep mysteries gulfed in thy bosom be!

III.

Oh, the moaning Tide! Oh, the waters wide!
Rocked in thy cradle I love to ride.

Tempest and grave in thy surges may be;
Terror and charm have their home with thee.
Thou 'rt a spirit of light, when dimples thy face;
Thou 'rt a monarch of might, in thy rushing embrace;
Thou art motion and life—deep music, wild glee,—
Thou art vast and sublime, type of Infinity.
Unaltered thou rolledst when earth-life began,
When the mystical garden held maiden and man.

IV.
Of the deep, deep Sea, of all souls I dream.
We have launched our ships on youth's warm stream.
Rich freighted with hopes, they traversed the main,
Some rudderless ones came never again.
We bend to our tasks, but at gloaming of day
We muse on our treasures afloat far away.
We watch for the gleam of the snow-white sails.
The storm-wind careers, and the last beam pales.
We weep and we pray—then submissively wait,—
And lo! our good ship safe enters the Gate!

They Watched the Sunset.

I.

LONG time they watched the sunset fill
    With molten glory all the vale,
The purple light of wooded hill,
    The snowy gleam of distant sail;

The well-marked mountain-path that wound
    From rock and forest far away;
Two wee ones tripping hand in hand,
    With glowing cheeks from romp and play.

The man's stern visage gentler grew;
    The book lay in his hand unread;
The low-voiced lady nearer drew,
    And turned her wistful face, and said:

II.

We twain have trod life's paths together
    In sweet June fields where roses blow,—
Through summer's fire; through autumn weather,
    Unto the chill of coming snow.

A long, long way; with many a tangle;
    With thorns that pierced our weary feet;
But side by side we've turned each angle,
    Entered the wide and smoother street.

Sometimes in our arms the pitying angel
    Left a cherub, and goldened our way.
A babe in the house, 't is a blessed evangel,—
    Life blossomed out with the beauty of May.

The scenes God pencils are wonderful Rembrandts.
    Our buds, soon frosted, withered away.
We solemnly cherished a fond remembrance,
    And low green mounds of precious clay.

On swept the years. Our lives were earnest,
    Nor loitered long by flowery streams.
Intent and resolute, thou discernest
    The possible danger of poet's dreams.

Now in our ripe and still September,
    Retracing the hills and the vales of our way,
Scarce seems the maid and wife we remember
    This soul that is hoping and sighing today.

She lived and she died. I seem as some other,
    Or whiter revive youth's earliest fires,
As hearts may strike more passionate drumbeats
    A moment before the pulse expires.

A bird in the dark, I peck at the window;
    Unknowing God's plan, I weave in His loom;
Wayworn and sad,—like yon child on the hillside,
    I am longing for love, and Home, sweet Home

We've almost finished our work together,
    Wrought and thought till the sun is low;
The mist-wreath hides our path to the River,
    But Fate alarums, and we must go.

Whether we've grasped the plan eternal,
　　Garnered the lore of the centuries long,
Or, ceasing to cope with the awesome Supernal,
　　Birdlike sat, and warbled our song;

Whether we've won the goal of ambition,
　　Carved a record above the rest,—
Or gained the coveted dearer fruition
　　Of sacred home love, sweetest and best;

Whether with strife and long disappointment
　　Bitter, we hung over nature a pall;
Whether our pain was an odorous ointment,
　　Making us sweeter and kinder to all,—

Side by side we have moved to life's sunset.
　　Day is hastening swift to its close
'T is best to clasp hands, be rev'rent and gentle,
　　Till twilight usher to dreamless repose.

Rest.

AFTER the worker's day,
    Welcome at last, release.
After the long and toilsome way,
    Sweet household rest and peace.

After perturbing care,
    After the crowded room,
Welcome the calm and happy air
    Of love and trust at home.

After the grinding mill,
    Turning by night and day,—
The ceaseless tasks the mind that fill,
    And wear the strength away,—

After the strife of tongues,—
    The eyes that saw not clear,—
After the arts of hindering ones
    That wrung a silent tear,—

After responsive thrills
    For other hearts that ache
With vision of the awful ills
    That earth a Bochim make,—

The conflict almost o'er,
    With many a victory won,

We drift beside a tranquil shore
   Toward the declining sun.

Sweet rest for toilworn frame!
   God's peace for weary soul!
Blest liberty of hand and brain,—
   Dear love to crown the whole!

Bright sunset hour of life!
   My Indian-summer days!
With teeming good the season's rife.
   Great God, accept my praise.

Still would I sow the seed
   Of truth by pilgrim path,
To glow in beauty where men tread,
   And be an aftermath.

When crimson day departs,
   And hands their toiling end,
'T were sweet if deep on some fond hearts
   My name were graved—'Our Friend.'

I know not what may be
   When night of death is o'er;
But trust in love vast as the sea,
   A sea without a shore!

The Mother's Task.

I.

I HEAR that you are loved of God,
    And made a rich and happy mother;
A sacred tie; a tender joy;
    A love unlike all other.
In days to come, sweet baby-charms
    And winsome ways will be unfolding
But most, the soul within thy arms
    Thy soul will e'er be molding.

II.

A mother! Oh, what thoughts are thine,
    When love's clairvoyance lights the years,
And traces for thy boy the line
    He'll tread in joys or fears?
A mother! Fair may be his form,
    And cherub face, his rings of hair.
But what the stamp upon the man?
    And will his life be fair?

III.

A mother! Oh, what mighty power
    For good or ill dwells in that word!
For all the chords of that young soul
    By thee shall first be stirred.
Thy voice shall tune his heart to feel,
    Thy face shall be his open book,

And in thy most unguarded hours
    Deep in thy heart he'll look.

IV.

Now thou canst bend that baby will;
    But when to sturdy manhood woke,
Say, canst thou mold the flinty rock,
    Or break the giant oak?
A mother! 'T is the holiest trust
    To saintliest mortal ever given,
To train by purity and truth
    For purity and Heaven.

V.

Oh, envy not the ermined queen
    Her canopy of state unfurl'd,
For mothers rock in humble homes
    The nations of the world.
And destiny waits on their breath,
    Who train the young with tale or song.
For deeds of heroism and faith,
    Or—weakness, guilt and wrong.

VI.

A mother! Didst thou ever dream
    With what that mystic word was rife?
Dost shrink lest thou shouldst harm the boy
    Thou lovest as thy life?
Then on God's altar consecrate
    Thyself and all thou lov'st to Heaven,
And guard with prayerful, ceaseless care
    The jewel He has given.

In Memoriam.

ROSES blush upon the plain;
 Trills the lark on fragrant lea;
Blooms my heart's flower ne'er again,
 Hushed the one sweet voice for me.

Dimpled fingers, snowy brow,
 Violet eyes and shining hair
Under clay are hidden low.
 Earth has naught that seems so fair.

Long have been the days, and dreary,
 Since my darling sank to sleep.
Oft my heart is sad and weary,
 Failing heavenly tryst to keep.

But her spirit seems to hover,
 Angel Eva glorified;
And I think when life is over,
 I shall slumber by her side.

The Early Dead.

SHE had a brief and sinless lot.
Not soon her name will be forgot.
She burst the chrysalis of clay,
And soared to realm of perfect day.

Joy, mourner, joy! that thou hast given
Thy bird of paradise to Heaven.
That in thy lily, pure and white,
The Heavenly Gardener takes delight.

Little Eva.

OFT in fancy now I see her,
    With her winning childish ways.
With a light and fairy figure,
    And a sweet, unconscious grace.
Sunny ringlets softly flowing
    O'er a neck of stainless snow,
Soulful eyes like star-orbs glowing
    'Neath her high and thoughtful brow.

On each lovely, chiseled feature
    Guileless innocence appears;
Yet her infant soul is stirring
    With a thought beyond her years.
She knows not deceit or doubting,
    Faith and Love her heart enshrine.
Ah! fair cherub, sweet and saintly,
    Would such love and trust were mine!

Now she trips with airy motion
    To the open cottage door;
Gazes on the gorgeous sunset,
    Vale and woodland, bird and flower,
Till her speaking eyes grow dreamy,
    And her earnest face more bright,
And a glory seems to wrap her
    Like a spirit clothed in light!

O my darling! O my angel!
　　Lo, thy mother's yearning arms.
Let me clasp thee to my bosom,
　　Kiss and shield thee from all harms.
Put thy dimpled, dainty fingers,
　　Waxen fingers, round my neck.
Let me hear thy silvery singing.
　　Eva! sainted darling, speak!

All in vain! The vision fadeth,
　　Like a pageant in the air,
And a low mound in God's acre
　　Shows me Eva sleeping there!
Deep and dark the shadow gathereth,
　　And my aching heart more sore,
For I know that I shall see her
　　In this wide world nevermore!

Yet I bow at this affliction,
　　Stilling now my anguish wild.
Well I know that God's affection
　　Overgoes mine to my child.
But this life will seem more dreary,
　　And the world more dull and plain,
Till I find my sweet immortal
　　On the Golden Shore again'

Voices of Nature.

BRIGHT bird! that skimm'st the waters blue,
    And on the treetop rests thy wing,—
What is thy mission? Tell me true,
    Is life to thee a gladsome thing?
A burst of music rippled clear.
    The bird laughed out in pearls of song,—
'Part of my mission is to cheer!'
    'To cheer! to cheer!' rang loud and long.

'I help my partner weave our nest,
    And while the embryo she broods,
I troll the strains she loves the best,
    That charm the sylvan solitudes.
'T is joy to fill each birdling's mouth;
    God doth their feathery coats prepare.
We steer like princes to the South,
    When Northern groves are chill and bare.'

O honey-bees! why toil ye so
    All day amid the fragrant clover?
Ye have your fill from flower-bell,
    Why store the nectar'd sweetness over?
'We cannot pause. We have our laws
    We're part of noble Nature's plan.
Were we to shirk, we'd spoil the work
    So marvellous, so prized by man.'

Sweet flowers!, that neither toil nor spin,—
  In more than Tyrian dyes arrayed, —
Why blush so deep, when all unseen
  In mountain dell or lonely glade?
For eye of God, who beauty loves,
  And sows it with a lavish hand;
That man may find, where'er he roves,
  God's finger-prints upon the land.'

While pondering these answers o'er,
  Some merry houseflies past me flew.
'We're scavengers,' they buzzed, before
  My quaint attempt to interview.
Since bird and bee and flower-gemmed sod
  Benevolent behest obey,
Shall man, in image like a God,
  Less joy to nobly serve than they?

Baby Grace.

'TIS o'er. I've seen thy face, my angel daughter,
  Now mirrored but in dreams.
Thou wert a star that trembled on the water,
  Then hid its timid beams.

Long had each glowing hope, each gorgeous vision,
  Caught richest hues from thee.
Methought thy nurture were a happy mission,
  A favored destiny.

Thou cam'st,—the best belov'd and long expected;
  But not to linger here.
So frail and fair, we knew thou wert elected
  To fill a higher sphere.

Pure as a dewdrop to the skies exhaling,
  Thy spirit passed away,
While we, with tears and anguish unavailing,
  Hung o'er thy precious clay.

Oh, it is hard to yield the hopes once cherished,
  And feel that all is o'er;
Yearning for grace and beauty that have perished,
  And will return no more.

For other mothers, love hath fond caresses,
  The dear delights of home,

Sweet prattle, winsome glances, cherub kisses,
    And riper joys to come.

But I may not behold thy fine unfolding,
    The child a maiden grown;
Nor see in beauty's shape thy spirit molding,
    For God hath claimed His own.

To walk unmurmuring, yet bereaved and lonely,
    Must be my earthly lot;
Still humbly trusting, not for sorrow only,
    Nor vainly I have wrought.

'T is not in vain to bear a child for Heaven!
    Life's painful paths untrod,
At once a blest eternity is given,
    Commensurate with God.

There *lives* our Grace, and with celestial pity,
    Perchance, regards our state;
Waiting until we reach the shining city,
    To ope the pearly gate.

Pet Charlie.

TWICE from our cottage of roses
    The spoiler had stolen the bloom,
And we wept by a blighted roof-tree,
    For beauty lost and perfume.

But the loving, all-wise Father
    On the flowerless stem hath smiled.
Again it blushes in crimson,
    Once more we enclasp a child!

Oh, joy so long denied us,
    Oh, ecstasy of bliss!
What's purer than child embraces,
    Or sweeter than boyhood's kiss?

His soul-lit eyes are radiant,
    He has brown, brown locks of hair.
His murmured "My own dear mother"
    Is music in my ear.

He comes a dancing sunbeam,
    Glimmering in and out;
Waking the household silence
    With boyhood's laugh and shout.

And yet his ways are gentle,
    Loving his book full well;

Locking within his youthful breast
Much more than he will tell.

Some winds have blown over him roughly,
    Some waves have whitened life's sea;
But all he has felt of sorrow
    Makes him but dearer to me.

By the deathless love of a mother,
    That thrills at the babe's first moan,
By tenderest ties of affection,
    I know he is all my own.

What thoughts in our bosoms are swelling,
    What hopes resurrected arise,
While we mark his grave, manly bearing,
    Or gaze in his eloquent eyes!

Love pierces the dim, distant future,
    And paints him to manhood grown,
Perhaps our staff and beautiful rod,
    For Age to lean upon.

But often we silently tremble,
    Faint with a secret fear,
Recalling our castles that crumbled,
    And the dead of many a year.

Blest Savior, we ask for our darling,
    Not long life, nor riches, nor fame;
But mold him into Thy likeness,
    And write Thou in Heaven his name.

The Robin by My Window.

CLOSE by my chamber window,
    I can reach at will,
    While sitting quite still,
The boughs of an apricot-tree,
    Where's the snug little nest
    Of a Robin Redbreast,
As cunning as cunning can be!

'T was built by a wise little mason,
    With twigs and fine grass,
    On a Sunday, alas!
She knew not the Decalogue, so let it pass.
    Then rounded with care,
    'T was quite finished there.
    Soon peeping over,
    We faintly discover,
With eager eyes, though with slight surprise,
    Three dainty, wee eggs
    Of the loveliest green
    That ever was seen,
And o'er them the brooding bird carefully flies.

The trees are aflame with bloom.
    The days are rapidly flitting.
    Still she is sitting, sitting,
That fond, watching mother-heart, patient and true;
    With black-beaded glances

For hostile advances;
Her nest ne'er forsaking,
Nor respite taking,
Save her morsel partaking, and sipping the dew.

What patience, and faith and love
That beautiful bird,
With plumage unstirred,
Is teaching us, often from duties deterred!
That an embryo dwells
In those green little cells,
Those bonnie wee shells,
Though never beheld, her nature foretells.

Though little she knows of the calendar,
And the time may seem long
To a creature of song,
Her love outbalances every fear.
Oh, a mother's heart
Is the most like that
Of the great brooding Spirit, that guards us here,
Of aught we shall know
Till skyward we go
And God's glory, full-orbed and effulgent, appear.

Suspense and Relief.

WEEP, heavens, until your starry eyes
    Are quite put out with tears,
And deeply drape with ebon dyes
    Where Luna's face appears.

And spread, O sympathizing Night,
    Thy shades o'er Nature fair;
Let gloom and darkness brooding sit
    Upon th' affrighted air.

For on my heart, as on the land,
    There lies a heavy pall;
And in life's wildering dark I stand
    Against an iron wall.

Enclosed behind, beside, before,
    I cry anear the grate,—
'Some loving angel, ope this door!'
    I wait—and wait—and wait.

Amid the awful hush I hear
    No heart that beats with mine;
No footfall bringing human cheer,
    No arms that round me twine.

Alone I wrestle with my fears,
    As in the garden He,

Who prayed, and wept with bloody tears,
    And unshared agony.

I could not tell to happy hearts
    The pain that thrills my own.
But o'er and o'er my burden sore
    I bear to God alone.

A wild suspense, a fear of wo,
    A dread of what may be
For one, to whom love's channels flow
    As streams that seek the sea.

Day after day, till weary weeks
    Of heartache now are gone,
I've looked expectant of some sign
    From a beloved one.

Oh, does he toss, the livelong night,
    Some fevered bed of pain?
Or sleeps he marble cold and white,
    Never to wake again?

Or, worse, in some mysterious hour
    When walks Hell's spectered host,
Oh, fell he 'neath the tempter's power,
    And sin's doomed threshold crossed?

Beleagured by each torturing fear,
    A very coward grown,
I call the fateful message near,
    Yet dread the message known!

Buried within this living tomb,
    O Lord, how long to stay?
Oh, let some pitying angel come
    And roll the stone away!

Yet, while Thou givest ashphodel
    And wormwood for my food,
Grant heavenly *patience* still to wait,
    And *faith* to own Thee good.

After the night, the glad morn breaketh.
After the snow, the spring flower waketh.
After long thirst, the fountain slaketh.
    So the white dove of Peace came to me!

Out of the depth of o'er-anxious surmising
My plaint unto heaven was hourly arising.
'T is turned to a pean of mercy surprising,
    And love, which adoring I see.

My far-away darling from falling God keepeth,
The angels keep vigil while sweetly he sleepeth.
He toileth and reapeth, and smileth, not weepeth.
    I sit by my hearthstone content.

Take heart for your burdens, O maidens and mothers.
Still labor and plead for the wanderers and brothers.
Then peacefully trust. God's ways, and no others,
    Are perfect, whate'er the event.

By the Cradle-Side.
[A young mother's reverie during a storm.]

DAY'S flickering sunlight has faded to shadow.
A clamorous gale is on forest and meadow.
There's a ceaseless roar from murmuring pines,
And the bird's nest rocks in quivering vines.
The dead leaves sail through the eddying air,
The loud thunders mutter, the red lightnings glare.
But I fear not the storm in its deafening glee,
While husband and nestling are safely with me.

Oh, ever the voice of my baby-girl seems
Sweeter than music that floats in my dreams.
Oh, ever the glance of her love-beaming eye
Has a halo no flash of the diamond can vie.
Her slight, winsome figure, with soft, sunny curls,
Has a lovelier grace than a shower of pearls.
And her face wears a beauty, I've thought, when she smiled,
Like that which adorned Madonna's blest child.

Then dearer than palace, the love-lighted room,
Where the flower of my heart is unfolding its bloom;
Where the bird of my bosom is singing her song;
Where the light of my life brings rapture along.
Let the tempest sweep on, there's an inner shrine here,
Where the vestal light burns ever warmly and clear,—
'T is affection's true altar, our own little cot.
Do what thou wilt, Father,—but, oh, harm it not!

Oh, what could earth offer, on land or on main,
To one ever pining for loved ones in vain,—
Whose heart is a pathway all bleeding and crushed,—
Whose most cherished idols have crumbled to dust?
For wounds such as these the earth has no balm.
Such billows of grief only Jesus can calm.
Faith sees the loved child on the glorified shore,
Not lost altogether—but gone just before!

Yet the mourner bereft has a sorrow for years.
There are nights of wild yearning and moments of tears,—
Quick thrills at the sound of a much-loved name,
And a ringlet or toy makes the heart bleed again.
Thank God that an angel still sleeps in my arms.
May sin never sully her blossoming charms.
When the night of life ends, may the child of my love
To her mother be clasped, in the sweet Dawn above!

The Spinster.

SHE sat beside the hearth fire,
    For it was chill November,
And fell to musing as she watched
    The slowly dying ember.
Her heart was calm, that once had glowed
    With love's impassioned flashes.
She only thought how like that fire
    Some hopes had turned to ashes.

Outdoor among the maples
    The fitful gusts were blowing,
And all the gold and scarlet leaves
    Were on the highway strewing.
The birds that piped in Maytime
    Had flown away together,
And sought the sunny Southland
    Before the snowy weather.

No more their liquid music
    Would thrill in pensive gloaming,
As once they sang in days gone by,
    When One with her was roaming.
Hark! Sings a bird this moment,
    In sweet and tender snatches,
Upon the sunny shingles,
    Near where she stands and watches.

Dear bird! how sweet thy pleading,
    When all have gone beside!
The last bird of the Autumn,
    Thou hast not fled, or died!
Take heart, O lonely spinster,
    Or gallant suiter gray,—
Though summer friends have scattered,
    One still may cheer thy way.

Stanzas Inscribed to a Young Lady.

AS gazing on a tress or flower,
    Love's sweetest memories oft awake,
Thus haply may this souvenir
    Be cherished for my sake.

'T were meet on friendship's shrine to lay
    The ripened fruitage of the brain;
Some sheaves of Truth, where thou couldst stray,
    Gleaning the golden grain.

Yet take this bunch of violets blue,
    Breathing the odors of the spring,
Which I have culled, sweet friend, for you,
    Though slight the offering.

It is the time of rippling rills,
    Of genial airs and bursting buds;
And rich, delicious music thrills
    Through Nature's solitudes.

The thrush melodiously pours
    In greening groves her varied lay.
The wild bees hum, and the white dove soars
    To her cooing mate away.

Oh, pleasant days! when love and mirth,
    Like sprites of beauty, roam abroad;
And as a chrysalis old Earth
    In splendor bursts her shroud.

Thou, too, my friend, art in life's spring.
    The sun of love on thee hath shone.
For thee the rose is blossoming,
    Its thorns almost unknown.

Joy lends thy soul her shining wings,
    And daydreams sweet as brooklets run.
The air with gladsome music rings
    And hope allures thee on.

Yet storms will burst on nature's bloom,
    And bleak will grow the autumn day;
No more be heard, amid the gloom,
    The birds that sang in May.

Yet mourn not spring's departed grace.
    Lo! harvest's richer wealth remains.
Some greater good in beauty's place
    Our Father oft ordains.

Symbol of life! Our budding joys
    Are often doomed to early blight.
'Neath fortune's frown we miss some voice
    That warbled 'neath its light.

We hear not now the thunder-cloud
    That may be gathering in the west.
We cannot see a coffined shroud
    Around the form loved best.

We only know our Lord employs
    Suffering as mercy in disguise.
E'en from the ashes of our joys
    Some nobler growth may rise.

Thou who wouldst close thine autumn days
    As flower-bells shut at set of sun,
With noble deeds and gentle ways
    Thy course of duty run.

Oh, live not for thyself alone.
    Sow wide the seeds of truth and love.
A glorious harvest will be grown,
    And heaven be thine above.

Death of the Second-Born.

I.

' OH! sweetly sings the bluebird, where rosy spring hath been,
And fair the snow-white lambkin that gambols on the green,
And fresh the breath of roses that scent the flowery lea;
But sweeter far this precious babe, O husband dear, to me!'

II.

Thus spake a new-made mother, in soft and loving strain,
'Mid nature's tears rejoicing, like sunshine after rain.
' Sure, God will spare this darling. He took our earliest-
born;
He will not leave us now again so desolate and lorn.'

III.

But when a single hour had passed, a change crept o'er the
child,
Its feeble breathing died away, and she cried, in accents
wild,
' Oh, who is that pale form that stalks within the open door?
Is it the stern death-angel, and knocks he here once more?

IV.

'Are there not many households where one would less be
missed?
Where numbers crowd the scanty board, untutored and
unblest?

Are there not many little ones who grow to sin and crime,
Unless in mercy early borne from the wild haunts of Time?

V.

'Why does Death seek our one pet lamb, our only pretty flower?
We had been long alone, till this, love's latest, richest dower,
And she was sought in many a prayer; and, thanking our dear Lord,
We would have trained her for Himself, obedient to His word.

VI.

'She should have grown a noble woman, both loving and beloved.
Oh, must we drink this cup? Death, canst thou not be moved?
How can we ever be resigned? O Thou who gav'st Thy Son,
Help us while agonized to cry, Father, Thy will be done!'

VII.

Oh, hour of untold anguish! But the boon she craved is given,—
She sees her babes all glorified, and living still in heaven,
While on her spirit evermore such angel fragrance lay
As if she walked in Paradise and bore its air away!

The Empty Nest.

LAST month, amid the sheltering shade
Of a leafy locust near my door,
Two birds their tiny nest had made,
And sweetly singing flitted o'er.

Two timid, unfledged birdlings there
Oped their expectant mouths for food,
And tender twitterings woke the air,
And music filled the listening wood.

Now when I gaze among the leaves
Only an empty nest I see.
The birds are flown, the warbling gone,
And shivering winds make plaint to me!

My home is like that vacant nest,
Forsaken, desolate and still!
Last month such treasure it possessed
As made my cup of bliss o'erfill.

A babe lay near my raptured heart,
On whom my fondest hopes were flung.
Love gushed to her from every part,
Like wealth of myrrh on zephyrs flung.

Today I search each silent room,
One voice to hear, one face to see.
'T is hushed and lone! *My* bird has flown,
And a breaking heart sobs out in me!

Little Broomstick.

I.

AS you roam our modern Babel,
'Mongst. the ever-surging throngs,—
Here, where shout the shrill-voiced newsboys,—
 There, 'mid snatches of street songs,—
Now, where votaries of Fashion
 Promenade in rich attire,—
There, where steeds with engines gallop
 Flying at the cry of Fire!--
Now, where 'buses, teams and street-cars
 Block up traffic's busy way,
While the slow and ponderous drawbridge
 Holds impatient crowds at bay,—
Should you find at some street crossing
 Mite of girl, a tousel-head,
Sweeping—sweeping,—know 't is "Broomstick,"
 Thus she earns her daily bread.

II.

"Little Broomstick" her cognomen.
Quite a heathen, by this omen.
Hers no happy home and mother,
Telling of the Elder Brother,
Soft repeating sacred story
Of the Lord of life and glory.
Naught she knew of holy Jesus—
How He loves from sin to free us,
Clasps the children in His arms,

Blesses, shelters from alarms.
Little Broomstick,—'t is no fable,—
Dwelt within our modern Babel.
But no almond-eyed Celestial,
    In his josshouse bowing down,
Was a more benighted pagan
    Than this waif of Christian town.

III.

Scanty food and long exposure
    Made the wee maid weak and wan.
One day from the crowded crossing
    Little Broomstick's face was gone.
To the hospital they bore her;
    Christmas bells were ringing out,
Christmas trees with gifts were laden,
    "Merry Christmas" was the shout.
"Broomstick" knew of furry Santa,
    With his pack and reindeer steeds,—
How he filled the children's stockings
    While they slept upon their beds.
He had naught for the street sweeper,—
    Gay old Santa loved her not;
Brought his toys down rich folks' chimneys,
    But the poor he quite forgot.
So it seemed to this pale sufferer,
    Weeping, lonely, in her cot.

IV.

But the matron bent above her,
    Laved and soothed each aching limb;
Gently told of God the Giver,
    And the Babe of Bethlehem;

Told of song of angel heralds
  Ringing through heaven's arches then,
'Glory in the highest! Glory!
  Peace on earth, good will to men.'
How the Christ-child dwelt obedient
  To His saintly mother dear.
How, a man, He went forth healing,
  Teaching, blessing everywhere,
Living sweeter, nobler, grander
  Than e'er man had lived before;
And, though kinglier than all monarchs.
  Chose to dwell among the poor.

V.

Loving, blessing little children, -
  Pitying, changing evil heart,—
Comforting the penitent;
  Was maligned with cruel art,
Though no soul upon the sod
Walked so near and like to God;
Taught a gospel, pure, sublime,
That shall conquer every clime,
That shall outlast fleeting time!
What's true life? 'T is loving nobly,—
  Not thyself, nor sense, nor pelf,—
Chiefly God; thy Elder Brother;
  Then—thy neighbor as thyself.
Low the woman's voice, and tender,
  With the tale so old, yet new.
'This dear Jesus loved the whole world.'
  "Even me?" 'Yes, Broomstick, you!
Yet men hated, crucified Him,
  Nailed Him on th' accursèd tree.
But He lives! He loves! and ever

With Him all His friends shall be!'
Deep these truths sank in the child-soul,
　　Much were pondered through and through.
'T was so blessed—'t was so joyful,—
　　Oh, that all the people knew!
And the pale, pinched face grew radiant,
　　Lying on the white-robed cot,
And the sweet eyes filled with pity
　　For the many knowing not;
And she longed to tell the story
　　Which such peace to her had brought.

VI.

Her small hand she laid in Nurse's,
　　When th' attendant came, one morn.
'Nurse! I'm hav'n' right good times. *Did you
　　Know 'bout Jesus bein' born?*'
"Yes, I know," the nurse said. "Sh! sh!
　　Do n't talk.—Yes, it's in the book."—
'Did you? Oh, I meant to tell you.
　　Thought you did n't—from your look.'—
Nurse grew curious. 'How do I look?'
　　'Oh, like most folks—kind o' glum."
And her next words were an arrow,
　　Flying to the mark straight home:
'Should n't think you'd look glum, ever,
　　Knowin' Jesus Christ has come!'

Friend, how much to thee is Jesus?
Thou whose face is curved with scorn,—
Thou who lookest oft forlorn,—
Knowst ''bout Jesus bein' born?'
If within thee burns a light,
Let it make thy face beam bright,—
Let it gladden others' night.

At Duty's Gate.

I.
THOU who art ever present still,—
    Though billowy leagues between us roll,—
Await with me the blessed will,
    The will of God, Friend of my soul.

II.
Today we meet at Duty's Gate—
    Behind us the returnless past,
Its bitter, which we felt was great,
    Its heavenly sweet, that did not last.

III.
Stern Fate doth stand, with key in hand,
    To lock the heavy gate between.
Thou must go forth,—I stay behind,—
    And we may never meet again.

IV.
Where duty calls the brave must be,
    My king, my hero,—though we part.
Heav'n has our highest fealty.
    I school—till it permit—my heart.

V.
Not mine to tempt thee from the right,
    Who love thee—love thee—love thee, Dear.

I need but one fond word to light
  Each darkly separating year.

VI.

One word—one look—hand claspt in hand,
  All doubt removed, all pain, all fear.
(Sweet spirits! hovering gently by,
  Pity, if nature makes outcry.)

VII.

Then strong to part at Duty's Gate,
  Thou unto noble, happy years,—
I still to toil, to hope, to wait,—
  Till one our lives, or done with tears.

God's World.

I.

WHEN green grasses are upspringing
 After winter's shrouding snow,—
When the rivulets are singing,
 Gaily dancing as they go,
When the robin's strain is ringing,
 And the skies are all aglow,—
When earth seems a new creation,
 Full of beauty, life and love,—
When the heart, like feet to music,
 With accordant joy doth move;
When soft winds sweet scents are bringing
 From the banks where spring flowers blow,
When fond arms to us are clinging,—
 When our plans no crossing know,—
Oh, 't is easy to believe
 This is GOD'S WORLD where we live!
Sweet it is in springtime's splendor
 God's all-glorious thoughts to trace;
Sweet to gain from lines so tender
 Glimpses of His lovely face;
Sweet to own Him our defender,
 Blissful moored within His grace.
Doubt its somber flag has furled!
Sweet is life! This is GOD'S WORLD!

II.

When there's no more emerald glory,—
 When the stubble-fields are bare,—

When the winter, grim and hoary,
    Breathes his frost-chill on the air,—
When the trees their creaking branches
    Beat against a leaden sky,—
When the hearth is still and lonely
    For one face no longer nigh,—
When thy hopes like leaves are flying
    While the blast goes howling by,
When the mills of care are turning,
    Grinding, ceaseless, day by day,
And thy soul for rest is yearning
    Lest they grind thy life away,—
When thy brain, long overwrought,
    Pictures forth some unknown bale,
As, if by the proud forgot,—
    As, if roof and bread should fail,—
When, by fears disquieted,
Thou dost sigh upon thy bed,—
Soul! that with an honest heart
Strives to do thy humble part,
Bid each anxious thought depart.
Doubt, thy treason-flag be furled!
For it is a good God's World.

III.

Never God a soul forgot.
Let Him choose thy earthly lot.
He will better plan for thee
Than if thine the choice should be.
Hast thou, mother, ne'er denied
Hurtful sweets from babes that cried,
Plotting still some glad surprise
That should greet thy darling's eyes?
'Neath the sod there's life still beating,—

Soon the resurrection hour.
Nature, lovely, palpitating,
Shall burst forth to perfect flower.
Thou shalt see the heart of gold,
Glories that can ne'er be told.
Thou art more than lily-bell;
Trust Him who attires it well.
On His palms thou 'rt graven fair;
He will make thy cause His care.
Ways severe thou canst not know
Are His rootlets under snow.
Trust to find them, by and by,
Precious to thy heart and eye.
Faith, thy banner be unfurled!
All is well. THIS IS GOD'S WORLD!

One More Day.

ONE more day—perchance thy last.
Soul, watch well till it be past.
Spend it as thou wouldst if Death
Should tonight arrest thy breath.

Each day brings its freight of care,
Something more to do or bear.
Faithful serve, that set of sun
Shine upon good work well done.

Sweetly bear when trials come.
Answer gently, else be dumb.
Only *one* day's burden bear;
Trust Tomorrow in God's care.

Is thy portion grievous, sore?
Son of God hath suffered more.
Lift thy heart for help divine;
Heavenly succor shall be thine.

Naught befalls by accident.
All is for thy welfare sent.
Winds and rains but make the tree
Firmer grow and greener be.

All around are storm-swept souls.
Passion raves and Pride controls,
Pour thine oil upon the wave.
Love, and love alone, can save.

The Visitor by Night.

THE night was dark; the hour was late.
In lighted room a lady sate,
Nor heard the footfalls of far Fate.

The household faces all were gone.
Sound, save her busy pen, was none.
I' the lonesome night she was alone.

Hearts may be stout in rosy day,
When town and field look blithe and gay,
And evil, cowering, hides away.

But in the dark, how timorous we!
How ghostly loom the stump, the tree!
How bold and base sin's troopers be!

Most helpless when upon our bed,—
Sleep's mandragora round us shed,—
In death's pale image we are laid!

The lady's mind from fear was free;
Her high thoughts bore her company.
Goodly companions pure thoughts be.

But striking clock and wearying brain
Admonished that the eve did wane,
And bade remit tired nature's strain.

Then every door she locked with care;
To snow-white couch did calm repair,
And breathed to God her childhood's prayer:

"Now I lay me down to sleep.
I pray Thee, Lord, my soul to keep.
If I should die before I wake,
I pray Thee, Lord, my soul to take;
And this I ask for Jesus' sake."

With all the world she was at peace.
She wished—whate'er her God might please.
From anxious dread her soul had ease.

Sleep soothed her with his poppy wreath.
She seemed,—so soft, so low her breath,—
A sculptured marble—or like death.

Silence, how deep! The clock strikes one.
The "wee, sma' hours" creep stilly on.
The awesome dark hath deeper grown.

One with a weird and solemn mien
Moves shadowy o'er the lonely green,
And through the lady's door goes in.

Oh, where are lock and barrier now?
Oh, is he friend or is he foe?
Or to a lover's tryst doth go?

Noiseless, unerring was his tread
To where she slept, on peaceful bed
'Sweet one, I do God's will,' he said.

THE VISITOR BY NIGHT.

One kiss he laid on cheek and brow.
She did not start at lips of snow.
More faint her breath did come and go.

Then all was still, and by her side
He sat him down till morning-tide;
And when her friends came, said, 'My bride!'

They saw the visitor was DEATH!
No human touch she sank beneath,
But, sleeping, sweetly ceased to breathe;

And passed, without a long decay,
From night of earth to heavenly day,—
From childhood's prayer to glory's lay!

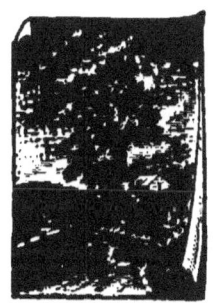

The Test of Poetry.

LIKE mountain peaks that lift their snowy brows
    Nearest to heaven's blue,
So grand old Homer, graceful Sappho, rose.
    So Dante, Milton, rare Will Shakspeare grew
To heights sublime; and still their luster glows
    With brighter glories in our centuries' view.

Yet beauty dwells as well in foothill's curve;
    And many a bell-like song
Not eagle's, soaring with unfaltering nerve,
    Doth wake sweet echoes in the valley long;
And hymns no tragic muse inspired oft serve
    To rouse or soothe the soul and turn from wrong.

Few are creators of transcendent verse.
    Yet some may dare to sing
Who are for genius fit interpreters.
    No Iliads or Infernos they may bring,
But at their bidding deep emotion stirs,
    And better purposes to being spring.

World's use is the true test of poet speech.
    All else will surely die.
To know one heart, in all its moods, will teach
    T'' interpret truly others' thought or sigh—
By song to lift the world's heart—were to reach
    The height of poets' immortality.

Twilight Musings.

IN the dim and pensive twilight,
    When the somber shadows fall;
When day's noisy babble ceases,
    And the nightwings brood o'er all;

When the humble task is ended,—
    Patient toil and passion's strife,—
Sitting by my lonely fireside,
    I bethink me of my life.

I have passed youth's rosy morning,
    With its hilltops flecked with gold,—
Felt the noonbeams fiercely burning,—
    Creeps my twilight gray and cold.

Swift the precious sands are dropping
    From the unfilled glass of time.
I must rouse, or lose a record
    Writ in words and deeds sublime.

Oh, the dreams, the aspirations,
    Fancy-tinted, scarce defined,—
Castles paved with rare mosaic,
    Fondly in my heart enshrined!

Sacredly have ye been cherished.
    Will ye crumble into dust?
Shall I reap, for all your sowing,
    Blossoms scattered by a gust?

Something of life's charm has faded,
    Like the mistwreaths of the morn;
And the thundercloud has shaded
    Brilliant prophecies of dawn.

While I muse, the years departed
    Pass with glancing sheen and shade;
Pilgrim feet with mine that started,
    Early tired, and lowly laid.

How the old, familiar faces
    Tremble on the dusky gloom!
How the unforgotten faces
    Start to life and fill the room!

I would clasp yon lovely cherubs,
    Babes that in my arms have lain;
But they vanish. I can never
    Win those shining ones again.

Oh, the aching and the longing!
    Oh, the dull and crushing pain!
Ah! there is a world of sorrow
    In the thought—It might have been!

Had they lived, what saintly beauty
    Might have crowned their ripened bloom!
Nay! they float in richer splendors—
    Heaven exchanged for sorrow's doom.

Praise to Thee, adored Redeemer,
    For the love my life has known.
Thou hast wounded, but in mercy.
    Be my chastened heart Thine own.

Thus amid the twilight shadows
Angel benisons descend.
Labor will seem holier, deeming
Heavenly visitants attend.

Waiting Near the River.

NEAR the Dark River I tearfully stand,
Awaiting my Lord's most solemn command,
To sail for the unseen, the Mystical Land.

One fond, lingering look I take ere I go.
Strong are the ties that bind me below,
But heaven is better and fairer, I know.

Farewell, then, to home, thou ark of my rest!
True love was the sweet singing-bird of my nest,
And Faith its guardian-angel confessed.

Farewell to bright dreams of merited fame—
Of thoughts that should glow with genius' pure flame.
Like castles they faded in air as they came.

Farewell to labor, most precious and sweet—
Gathering sheaves for the Master meet—
Casting crowns at the Savior's feet!

Farewell, then, to life, its hopes and its fears.
Ended its cares, its joys and its tears.
Thrice welcome be Heaven's celestial years.

Pitying Savior! one will be lone
When the friend from his side forever is gone.
Tenderly round him let Thine arms be thrown.

When the pathway of life grows rugged and wild,
Let memories come of companion and child,
And solace him, as though an angel had smiled!

A thrilling voice from the radiant shore,
And a form of grace, now woo me o'er.
I know that face for my heart's own flower!

Vision of loveliness! Oh, can it be
That shining immortal is beckoning me?
Child of my soul, I come unto thee!

Elysium of bliss! My mourning is done.
I float like a bird in the beams of the sun,
And the long-lost pearl of my bosom is won!

Father all-glorious! Thee I adore,
Who bearest our doves from earth's darkened door,
That they may be ours, in heaven, evermore!

Pressed Flowers from the Land of Long Ago.

The following seven numbers were composed between the ages of fifteen and seventeen, and have been revised by the author.

A Mother.

THE silvery fount may cease to flow,
   The floweret's hues no longer glow,
But all that's bright in heaven above
Is like a mother's quenchless love.
More constant than the stars that glow,
More pure than flakes of stainless snow,
More bright than rainbows e'en, that quiver
Upon a dark and mist-hung river,
A Mother's love must always be,
When in unsullied purity.
'T is Mother rocks our cradled sleep.
'T is Mother soothes us when we weep.
In time of sickness or of pain,
'T is Mother calms the weary brain.
And through the devious range of life,
In joy, in sadness or in strife,
A Mother still appears in view—
A woman, yet an angel, too!

My sister, lives thy Mother yet?
Oh, ne'er her precious words forget.
Prize every whisper of her voice,
And make her aged heart rejoice.
Be kind to Mother; though she's old,
Her sensibility's not cold,—
Though winters have around her fled,
And left their snows upon her head.

She soon may reach her heavenly home,
And thou be left to weep alone.
Then thou wilt miss her meek, mild face,
Her gentle smile, her quiet grace;
Wilt weep that thou didst strew her hours
With thorns, where should have been but flowers!

Thou hast kind friends around thy path
    While lives thy father, sister, brother;
But love like hers none other hath.
    O God! I thank Thee for my Mother!

The Soul's Quest.

OH, the soul cannot find in this wide world its rest.
Life's cares are consuming, its mirth is unblest.
Earth's pleasures are fading as dew-honeyed flowers,
That bloom but an hour in the loveliest bowers.

Then lay up your treasure in yon world of joy,
Where bliss is eternal, and naught can alloy;
Where music entrancing fills Heaven's high dome;
Where the loved and the long-lost will welcome you home.

Disillusion.

FRIENDS more dear than words can tell,
And friends that seem to love us well,
　　May fail when needed most.
May die, like flowers when summer's done,
Or change like tints at set of sun,
　　Betraying sacred trust.

Fame's charmèd waters wildly quaffed,
And Love's still more beguiling draught,
　　Oft leave a bitter taste.
Deluded we may drink the cup,
The heart's rich fragrance offer up,
　　Alas! to run to waste.

Friendship is often light as air,
And Flattery proves as false as fair,
　　And Youth's dear dreams depart.
E'en Hope, sweet angel, still has wings,
And sometimes soars, while yet she sings,—
　　What then is left, O heart?

Turn, yearning spirit, from the sod,
Thy wealth of love devote to God,
　　In nobler service given.
Tossed long on life's tempestuous foam,
Thou'lt find at last thy peaceful home,
　　And perfect love, in Heaven.

A Song of Cheer.

OH, never surrender your faith or your heart
    To the goblins of terror and sadness.
If a cloud is in view, there's a rainbow, too.
    Press onward, white soul, in thy gladness.

Remember, when pierced by the briars of life,
    The rosebud is near to the thorn,
And dreariest night oft bringeth the light
    Of fairest and loveliest morn.

Though sorrows encompass, and dangers attend,
    Though man passeth loftily by,
Yet never despond, for a change in the wind
    Will chase the dark fog from the sky.

These trials our Maker in wisdom ordained;
    They are destined to chasten or prove us.
We all should appear, like gold in the fire,
    More bright when the heat is above us.

Though fortune should frown, and thy fellows forsake,
    Or insidious rumors surround thee,
Yet live them all through; they will vanish like dew,
    If virtue be only around thee.

Then never despair; but rather endure,
    With stern and unfaltering soul;
Press onward still higher, to Heaven draw nigher,—
    Thy destiny God will control.

A Poet's Heart.

OH, a poet's heart is a sensitive thing;
A timid bird, with a fluttering wing;
A lyre whose chords are thrillingly sweet,—
Whose texture is fragile, its melody fleet.
When rudely 't is handled, the once flowing strain
Is turned from entrancing to discords of pain,
Till the harp whose sweetness delighted us ever
Lies shattered and silent, forever! forever!

Adieu.

ADIEU, sweet friends, The sad parting hour
Now comes o'er our spirits, like frost o'er the flower.
How mournfully like to some slow-tolling knell
The desolate sound of that one word, Farewell!
Broad rivers and plains our fortunes may sever,
On earth we may meet again never, O never!
Yet the Bird of Remembrance, a sweet, viewless thing,
Will hover around us and pleasantly sing
Of hours long past, and of friends whose forms
Seem ever to shine 'mid the dreariest storms.
Oh, may love's chain, now tearfully riven,
Still link us to God and each other, in heaven!

Premonition.

COME hither my harp! I will waken thy strain.
Sweet harmony's numbers should soften my pain.
Thy music oft gives me an exquisite thrill,
But life's emptied chalice thou canst not refill.
Alas! my harp is a fragile thing.
'T is a wounded bird, with a broken wing;
A garland of roses whose beauty is fled,
Still scenting the air with the fragrance they shed;
'T is a moonbeam that shimmers when daylight is gone;
A mountain's last echo, when trumpets are done;
A barque slowly drifting on night's cheerless sea;
An infant falling asleep in its glee;
A tone from melody's tenderest strain,
Which mounteth, then melteth in silence again.
'T is like beauteous birds, that heavenward fly;
'T is like all bright things that earliest die.

Poems of Special Occasions.

Reunion Poem.

[Read at the Annual Meeting of the Early Settlers of Lee County, Illinois, September 3, 1885.]

ALL hail! and welcome! yeomen, veterans, friends!
   Ye Early Settlers of the shire of Lee.
The benediction that from ill forefends,—
   The smile of Heaven,—rest on you royally,
   And mark in white this day in memory.
Ye toilworn chieftains of the clans, all hail!
   And venerated dames, thrice welcome ye!
Gathered from farm, from town, from hill, from dale,
Ye are the heroes for our poet's tale;
Sad were our meeting, should your presence fail.

Assembled in this goodly company,—
   This worthy seat of learning at our side,—
Fair Ashton, with the prosperous farms of Lee,
   Unrolling to our vision far and wide,—
   What more need modest mortal ask beside?
Thrift, order, peace, health and security!
And yet what contrasts from the early years,
So well remembered by these pioneers!
The hardships of the present shrivel when
Confronted with those met so bravely then.

Fresh from an Eastern home when you were young,
   By glowing tales of the Far West beguiled,
With long farewells your kindred's hands you wrung,
   To seek your fortunes in the prairies wild.

No railroads here those fifty years ago;
No bridge o'er slough. Travel was hard and slow.
The ox-team and the prairie schooner brought
To Illinois its old-time Argonaut.
Chicago was an embryo in the bud,—
A water-lily, sprung from marsh and mud.

In those primeval days when we came West,
Black Hawk but lately had been dispossessed.
Wild game roamed o'er the grassy plain,
Fair target for the marksman's aim.
You built your homes of log or Hoosier board;
They were but small, but held your little hoard.
Your neighbors then were few and far away;
But oh, what hospitality held sway!
What cheer! what helping hands! what kindly jest!
The good old days are gone that were so blest.

Up with the singing lark at earliest morn,
You broke the virgin sod, you dropt the corn.
At length, with summer's sun, your wheatfields rolled
A broad and billowy sea of yellow gold.
The harvester unknown, you 'cradled' then.
Indoors your good wives cradled little men!
Those lively chaps! how fast they came and grew!
You built the schoolhouse, and the chapel, too;
You built the future better than you knew!
The public school, the church, are towers of strength.
They make the state impregnable at length.

To politics you gave some sturdy thought.
Stood at the polls; your vote was never bought.
When baby prattlers suddenly grew dumb,
In some sequestered spot, where wild bees hum,

In meadow-grasses sweet, or clover bloom,
    All tenderly ye gave " God's acre ' room.
And so your hearts and granaries grew full.
    And so the villages like magic sprung.
And so you reared your mansions beautiful,
    And ponderous bells in high church-steeples swung.

One day the locomotive's whistle rent
    The stillness of the country atmosphere!
You saw, on iron rails, the first train sent,
    And then the world of travel all was here.
The hour would fail your bard to fitly tell
The wondrous changes that the land befell.
The civil war—its knells are in your hearts.
For some who bravely fell the teardrop starts.
But should you wish the fuller tale's repeating,
Come next year to the Early Settlers' meeting.

Then hail! and welcome! yeomen, veterans, friends!
    Ye Early Settlers of the shire of Lee!
The benediction that from ill forefends,—
    The smile of Heaven,—rest on you royally,
    And mark in white this day in memory.
Ye toilworn chieftains of the clans, all hail!
    And venerated dames, thrice welcome ye!
Gathered from farm, from town, from hill, from vale,
Ye are the heroes for the Muses' tale.
May heaven receive you when from earth ye fail.

For a Golden Wedding.

[Composed while waiting at a railroad depot.]

TWO youthful hearts, in days of old,
    At Love's sweet tale grew tender;
Love touched the hills of life with gold,—
    Love filled the air with splendor.

Full fifty years that wedded pair
    Have trod the way together,
Doubling the joys, halving the pain,
    In shine and cloudy weather.

Again the chime of wedding-bells
    Brings joy without restriction,
And crowds salute that veteran pair
    With golden benediction.

Oh, blessings on their aged heads!
    Serene be skies above them!
Their souls be calm with Heaven's peace,
    And cheered by those who love them.

And when life's gold grows dim and cold,—
    Still kept in Heaven's pity,—
May their glad feet walk golden street,
    And rest in Golden City!

Commemorative Stanzas.

[Read before the Chicago Congregational Ministers' Union, at the First Congregational Church, December 15, 1874.]

I.

THE weary year to his end draws near,
    And lies a-cold, on his frosty bier.
The holidays come, when the sons who roam
Find Mecca and shrine with the Old Folks at Home.
By the hearthstone bright of our Mother, tonight,
    A goodly band, we joyfully meet.
Some, seaward wandering from our sight,
    With a hearty 'Welcome home' we greet,
And tender voices and clasp of hands
For absence long shall make amends.

II.

Kindred in toil for our common Lord,
    Kindred in soul and in life's grand aim,
Heart beats to heart with a warm accord,
    And each in each may a brother claim.
Let gladness rule this festal hour,—
Let wisdom yield her priceless store,
And wit its iridescent ore,
And friendship cull her sweetest flower.
The banquet's spread with a royal cheer.
The children are home! Are we not all here?

III.

Is there a spot in the world so fair
That sorrow's shadow falls not there?

E'en now some woman is waiting without
Some wretch's return from his bacchanal bout.
Some orphan in rags, on the pavement below,
Shivers and quakes, with nowhere to go!
God pity them! pity them! care for us all!
This doomful year the funeral pall .
Twice darkened our sunshine! We own with a tear,
And a sense of loss—We're not all here!

When spring with its delicate bloom came on,
Each gem in our circle resplendently shone.
Their presence that cheered lies hidden below
The mold of the earth and the cold, cold snow.
The teacher revered,—of golden-mouth'd speech,
Brave thinker, yet gentle as woman to each,—
Another of queenly figure and mien,—
Ah! crowned by the angels too soon, I ween.—
They left us but mem'ries of all they have been.
There's a tremulous strain that thrills the ear.
'T is the sad refrain,—We're NOT all here!

We're not all here! Then closer draw—
    Snug up the circle while ye may.
Cherish more warmly, for ye know
    Some pearl may speedily drop away.
The heart of another ye may not guess
Nor know its need of tenderness.
In coming days, when ye shall meet,
There will be often a vacant seat.
God grant at last we may all appear,
And say, This is Heaven! WE'RE ALL, ALL HERE!

Hymns

Composed for and sung at the Quarter-Centennial Celebration of the General Congregational Association of Illinois, at Farmington, May 27, 1869.

Memorial Ode.

Tune — "America."

I.

O THOU all-perfect Lord,
By angel hosts adored,
    Thy praise we sing.
Humbly thy churches call,
Come, grace our festival,
Pour Thy rich wine for all,
    O Christ, our King.

II.

Back o'er the vista'd past
Our grateful eyes we cast,
    And trace Thy hand.
For seeds in weakness sown
See golden harvests shown—
Thy scattered saints have grown
    A num'rous band.

III.

The fathers, where are they,
True vet'rans of the fray?
    Heaven bless our braves!

Some rest from mortal care,—
Some still the harness wear,—
The almond in their hair
　　Its blossoms waves.

IV.

Our and our fathers' Lord,
By seraph choirs adored,
　　Wondrous and great!
Gathered from lake and plain,
We swell the suppliant strain,
God bless this fair domain—
　　God save the State!

Looking Forward: Or, The Land of the Forever.

Tune—"Shall We Gather at the River?"

I.

WHEN we cross the mystic river,
　　And our mortal life is o'er,
In the Land of the Forever,
　　Shall we gain the golden shore?
Nevermore with grief to quiver,
But beautiful and purified forever—
Nevermore with loved ones to sever—
　　Safe on that blissful shore.

II.

When the fateful books are opened,
　　And the judgment court is set,—

When each pastor with his people
  And a countless throng have met,—
Shall we hear the glad evangel
Of 'Well done, faithful,' from our dear Lord's angel?
Shall sweet welcomes greet us to the Crystal,
  Swelling our rapture yet?

III.

What if from the awful Presence
  Our reverseless doom should be,
'Faithless shepherds to my creatures,
  Ye have faithless been to Me!'
Could we bear the accusing faces
We never tried to mold to heavenly graces?
What if we should win the shining places,
  And starless our crown should be?

IV.

Savior, low we take our station.
  Hear the churches' fervent call.
Clothe Thy heralds with salvation,—
  Tongues of fire anew let fall.
Help us tell the touching story,—
The beautiful, the wonderful, true story,
How the loving Lord, the Prince of Glory,
  Died to redeem us all!

Hark! the Muffled Drums are Beating!

DIRGE FOR GENERAL GRANT.

Tune—"Hark, the Voice of Jesus Calling," by H. R. Palmer, page 8 of "The Gospel in Song."

I.

HARK! the muffled drums are beating,
 Soft and slow,
 Notes of wo.
O'er the brave chant love's last greeting,
 Ere we lay him low.
Deeper swells the lamentation,—
Low degree and lofty station,—
'T is the wailing of a nation
 For its Chief laid low!

II.

Ended now the weary marches,—
 Bivouack'd here,
 On a bier.
Sentry stars keep silent watches
 All the livelong year.
Spread his tent with roses blowing,—
Winter snowy whiteness strewing,
Flags of victory o'er him flowing,
 Who hath conquered Fear!

III.

Whence the people's vast devotion?
  Humbly born,
  Simply bred,
Loyal, brave,—in war's commotion
  He Columbia led.
Silent, firm;—mistake is human;—
Grand in action, one of few men,—
Warrior! hero! Christian! true Man!
  Laurels deck his head!

IV.

Now, with Peace' pure banner o'er thee,
  Sweetly rest
  On earth's breast.
They will emulate who love thee,
  East and mighty West.
When shall fade thy fame from story?
Not when soldier-sires are hoary,—
Ne'er while lives the Union's glory,—
  Land thou lov'dst the best!

New-Year's Day Salutation of the Carrier.
January 1, 1859. (Took the prize.)

TO our numerous friends and our patrons dear,
As the form of the Old Year vanishes fast,
And its swallow-like joys on light wings have passed
For pleasures the sweetest may not always last,—
    Your Carrier wishes a Happy New Year.

A Happy New Year! What visions it brings,—
Of gifts for the children of curious things,—
Of greetings of young hearts unfettered by care,
Of silvery laughter rung out on the air,—
Of joyful reunions of circles long broken,—
Of tearful adieus that are tenderly spoken;
And as days of the New Year pass dreamily by,
What pictures of sunshine or shade meet our eye!
Today, icy torrents and glittering snows.
Anon, singing rills and scent of wild-rose.
Next season, young song-birds will mount from the nest,
And infantile forms be by young mothers pressed.
Lips red as wet coral, and eyes of soft blue,
And velvety fingers with touch light as dew,
Will bring more delight to a fond parent's heart
Than earth's richest treasures could ever impart.
But a shadow will creep over many a wall;
Full many a loved one be laid 'neath the pall.
The beaming-eyed maiden with bridal wreath,
When a few months are past, may be sleeping in death.

For life's a kaleidescope,—turn it at will,
The scenes it presents are varying still.

'But, Carrier, what of the year that is dead,
    The old man forgotten and lone?'
Methinks you say. 'We are ling'ring to read
    Some record of what he hath done.'

To the burial-place of the monarch we go.
A tablet we rear for the king laid low;
His epitaph write, for his deeds we know.
Twelve daughters had he of varying charms.
Like a garland of flowers they drooped in his arms!
At dead of last night the youngest-born died,
And father and daughters lie side by side!

His career 'mid the nations was gorgeous and great—
An era to science and matters of state.
The bubble of wild speculation burst,
And meek-brow'd religion arose from its dust.
American commerce, that pond'rous machine,
With its numberless wheels turned by millions of men,
With its railroads, its steamships, its lightning expresses,
Its huge manufactures, its swift printing-presses,
Its star-spangled banner, on all seas unfurl'd,
Its field of adventure, as wide as the world,—
This fabric so vast felt a sudden sensation,
An electric shock to its very foundation.
God arrested this Babel of human pride,
And confusion and terror fell heavy and wide.
Blight crept on the fields—the markets declined,
Vast fortunes departed, like chaff in the wind,
Till the fair dome of commerce all prostrate lay
Like miniature houses of children at play,

Where with one falling brick all have toppled away.
The past should not teach us a lesson in vain.
It counsels a system of honorable gain;
Of patience, economy, honesty, skill,
And a Christian-like trust; and to commerce shall still
A pedestal broader and grander arise,
With a column of grace pointing up to the skies.

In the silence that followed that earthquake in trade,
Men, feeling their helplessness, sought divine aid.
The prayer-room was crowded at noonday and night,—
The Spirit descended—the blind saw the light;
And hundreds and thousands of stout hearts bowed,
And their burdens fell off at sight of the Lord.
In the landscape of time that revival will be
God's lighthouse from heaven on life's dreary sea!

  But hark! what hosannas of rapture are heard
   Rolling up from the Eastern main?
  While valley, and hilltop, and mountain and wood
   Re-echo the chorus again?

A pean in honor of science they sing,
For mind over matter again is king.
'Mid the surges of ocean the CABLE is laid,
And the harnessed lightning man's message conveyed.
Magnificent thought! culmination of art!
Two continents wedded, while widely apart!
Then ring out the anthem, sweep music's rich keys,
Unfurl our bright banner again to the breeze.
But permit us to whisper, kind friends, in your ear,
That union of realms, there is reason to fear,
Is proving unhappy, for the wits do say
They've exchanged not a word since the bridal day!

The Old Year brought us a visitant rare—
A comet emerging from vast fields of air.
Nightly it hung out its luminous train,
Then vanished from sight for ages again,—
Its history, essence and object unknown,
Through abysses of space, a wandering one.

In politics, too, there has been much commotion.
Buchanan has shown to the South his devotion.
' Little Dug' he refuses to own as a brother,
And Democracy's leaders oppose one another.
The Republican phalanx, a veteran host,
Must assuredly triumph, if true to its trust;
For Freedom's our national watchword and sign,
And tyranny's reign must surely decline.
Since sorghum's successful, we'll make our own sugar,
And no longer need the purchase of Cuba!

. . . .

In the circle of blessings we name but one more—
The weekly paper you greet at your door.
A noiseless attendant it lies in your hand,
But pours out its treasures from many a land.
A friend to all classes and orders of men,
It has honestly striven the right to maintain.
If the paper has pleased you, remember the printer,
And send your subscriptions in time for the winter.

 Farewell to the Old Year! a hero at rest.
  All hail to the happy New Year!
 Ring out, merry bells, your wildest and best,
  Let the welkin resound with your cheer!

The book of the future what mortal can know?
Its pages are spotless as untrodden snow;

We must fill up the record as onward we go.
Then trace it in lines of beauty and light,
In words of affection, in deeds for the right.
Conquer thyself! Such a triumph is grander
Than to be of two hemispheres highest commander.
Be faithful to God and humanity here,
And thine shall be Heaven's immortal New Year!

New-Year's Address, January 1, 1860,
[Took the Prize.]

KINDLY greeting, friends, we bring you, while we hail
the newborn year,
Carols for the infant monarch, for the dead one drop a tear.
Past a twelvemonth's lights and shadows, springtime bloom
and summer glory;
Past its harvest wealth and autumn tint, December chill
and hoary;
Past its mocking hopes and witching scenes; past bliss too
sweet to last.
Then welcome, welcome to the New Year; tender farewells
to the past.

Yet would we gather up its treasures and its lessons ere
we part;
Pressing, as roseleaves in a book, its fragrant memories in
the heart;

Sketching its living pictures in the rare art-chamber of the
    brain;
Thinking one gush of its old music will recall all back
    again.
Our early loves and joys should be impearl'd immortal in
    the soul,
A legacy for later years, making life ever beautiful.
Unheeding this, men drink but half the nectar of their
    honey'd cup.
'T is memory, as well as hope, that fills life's golden chalice
    up!

Hear, then, the old year's record, writ on history's impartial
    page.
Freedom from tyranny was the momentous question of the
    age.
Europe, whose proudest thrones have a volcano threat'ning
    at their base,
Shook with convulsions stirred, and haughty monarchs trem-
    bled for their place.
The contest maddened at Magenta and on Solferino's plain,
And the fair, flower-gemm'd earth was strewn with stiffened
    corses of the slain.
Italy and Hungary, long trodden bleeding in the dust,
Were doomed by Villafranca's peace to have their hopes
    of freedom crushed.
Yet 'mid the deepest darkness let them bravely watch the
    dawning light,
Knowing no traitorous peace can long endure, not founded
    on the right.

But hark! what thrilling strains are wafted from the green
    isles of the sea?

'T is Erin's thousands shouting out the rapturous anthem
    of the free.
Though vassals of a foreign court, yet now released from
    sin's control,
Theirs is the highest form of liberty, the freedom of the
    soul!
O'er the blue Atlantic waters comes the din of strife again,
Tumult waxing hotter, fiercer, on Virginia's proud domain.
Let them hang the brave, misled man courts and scaffolds
    cannot move,
All the world applauds the martyr, sacrificed for crime of
    love!
And his death shall prove the birthday of a people strong
    and free,
And his planting have its harvest in a nation's jubilee!

The scene is shifted. Far away in Arctic regions and 'mid
    polar snows,
And weird, unbroken solitudes, where venturous mortal
    seldom goes,—
Where night and silence, sisters twin, for centuries divide
    the sway,—
Where mystery broods specter-like, and science, baffled,
    yields the day,—
A lonely cairn reveals the fate of hapless Franklin and his
    crew.
No more his home and native land shall greet the gallant
    hero's view.
No more the form he saw in dreams be fondly clasped to
    his side.
Long years have passed, thou watching widow, since thy
    loved and lost one died!

Wail, sighing winds, your saddest dirge, and weep, thou
fitful, sobbing rain,
For grace and beauty, wit and genius, that can never come
again.
Behold, the prince of nature dies, whose eye the world's
arcana traced;
But "Cosmos" shall enshrine the name of gifted Humboldt
uneffaced.
And still another orb declines in softened splendor in the
West:
Full of successes and of toils, the Christian Olmsted goes
to rest.
Prescott and Hallam, honored men, who chronicled the ages
past;
And Choate, whose winning eloquence a gorgeous memory
will last;
Genial Leigh Hunt and graceful Irving, both with years
and honors crowned;
And Mann, the wise and faithful friend of education ever
found;
And sainted James, the last and best, to whom such sweet-
ness here was given,
That where he went, his soul diffused the balmy atmosphere
of heaven:
All these have crossed the darksome valley, and the icy
river trod,
And while the old year rolled its round, their spirits home-
ward went to God.

Our fair village still rejoices in her growing thrift and fame;
Only rum and license sully the escutcheon of her name.

. . . .

Here we close a twelvemonth's drama; but the world will
    never know
All the varied tragedies that thrilled life's inner current
    through,—
The newborn bliss that made a moment sweeter than a
    common year,—
The restless yearning for some darling torn from love's
    embraces here.
Still we know these chastenings are God's dear angels in
    disguise.
Lifted on their gentle wings, oh, may our weak affections
    rise.
May we all next year remember victories gained o'er sin
    and wrong,
And, when ends life's bleak December, sing in heaven the
    New-Year song!

Twenty-Eight.

IT is a glorious autumn eve. The sky
 Has the deep, clear-cut brilliancy it wears
When rains are over; while delicious airs,
Fragrant from kissing flowers of richest dye,—
Whose bloom outvies the early tints of spring,
As new wives oft eclipse the shrouded old,—
Caress me with exhilarating touch.
My soul is tremulous with thought tonight,
As violets o'erfull of pearly dew.
I yield the hour to Fancy's spell, and lo!
Unbidden memories trooping start to life.
Again I see the scenes of early years.
I hear the voices that have long been still,
And feel the former thrills of joy or pain.
Dimly arising from the twilight gloom,
The ghost of my departed hours appears,
Waves her weird finger backward to the past,
Its buried opportunities and joys,—
Then, slowly fading, murmurs 'Nevermore!'
I heed the mystic word that warns me of
My vanished prime. Today I'm Twenty-Eight.

Of all I hoped to accomplish much remains
To do. The fair ideal still I see,
Of spirit fine, and strong, and self-possessed,
And rounded in a perfect womanhood.
'T is far away, shrined saintlike, in the clouds.
Methinks we are but children larger grown,

Chasing the rainbow we can never reach.
In youth we dream and plan. For coming time
Looks long, as travelers deem the hills they climb.
How short the retrospect! The telescope
That magnifies in childhood we invert
To view the past. In later life appears
More swift the flight of our revolving years.

I would my days were writ with more accomplish'd
Good, more service done humanity,
More deeds for God. Though I've not idle been,
I know sometimes I have not toiled aright,—
Too much have cared for human praise or blame,—
Not always wisely spent the precious hours.
Yet let me ne'er forget the humblest task,
If done for Christ's sweet sake, is nobler than
The greatest done for self. The motive elevates.

'T is very fair tonight. Yet stormy was
The solemn hour that ushered me to life,
Portending truly that the fragile barque
Thus wildly launched on Time's tumultuous depths
Should sometimes drift on troublous seas. And while
My soul is full of melody tonight,
And lifts adoring thanks to bounteous Heaven
For gifts unnumbered, and my path hath lain
Far more in shine than shadow, yet some thorns
Have deeply pierced my heart, and so its gush
Of song may sometimes have a strain of wo.

Upon the brow of wifehood God had set
His holiest seal, and crowned me Mother. Ah!
A sweeter name and prouder throne than queen!
How dear that only birdling of the nest!

To me the star of hope, the sun of home,
Pearl, rose and lily, cherub, all in one!
What thousand thoughts into existence sprung!
A world of love appeared,—then, sunk from sight,
And all grew dark where had been clearest light.
Yet still I bless the Hand that dealt the blow.
'T was done in purest love. I feel it so.
The sinless child is safe, that to my heart was given,
And suffering sanctified makes meet for heaven.
The cross and crown are linked by God's behest.
The sweet and bitter! and 't is surely best.
The path to glory is the martyr's stake.
For freedom's sacred cause some hearts must break,
And nations' death-throes grander empires make.

The future yet enfolds a promise bud.
With chastened hopes and labor-strengthened hands
I gird me for the coming work. There's much
To live for in such times as these, when right
And wrong are arming for the deadly fight;
When Liberty—our precious Isaac—on
The altar lies, the blade of doom o'erhung.
God send some other sacrifice to turn
His just displeasure from our guilty land.
God save the nation, furnace purified,
With nevermore a slave to clank his chains.

Woman must cheer the warrior to the fray
With smile heroic, though with secret pain;
Must trim the homelight, and breathe many a prayer;
Train a race worthy of their patriot sires,
Loyal to truth and God. Let each fulfill
Her sacred trust, and better days will come!

Thanks.

ACCEPT sincerest thanks, kind friends,
For the rich gift you bring.
A Cowper sang the sofa's praise;
This silken robe I sing,
And tender thoughts in coming days
Will for the givers spring.

Beauty and Use alike commend
This offering unto me.
'T is well, sweet friends; these charming twain
Divinely wedded be.
For God, who formed the mighty main,
Tints each shell of the sea!

O maidens fair! in the loom of Fate
Your lives are weaving to-night.
Dark threads of sorrow and pain are warped
With stripes of golden and white.
Your words, your deeds are spinning the thread.
Oh, make it strong and bright!

The ravages of time will soil
This soft and lustrous dress.
And so must fade your forms, now full
Of youth and loveliness.
Oh, then be yours the spotless robe
Of Christ's own righteousness.

Ten Circling Years.

[For a Tin Wedding.]

TEN circling years, in storm and shine,
    In cold, in summer weather,—
Ten years of love, true wife of mine,
    We've trod life's paths together.
Ten whirling years! Not very long,
    But, oh! enough for changes!
What images around me throng,
    As memory, wakened, ranges.

I see thee—in the witching hour
    When we were youth and maiden,—
In meadows green, a pure white flower,
    With thine own sweetness laden.
I see thee stand in village school,
    My blue-eyed Golden-Hair,
And mark thy gentle, kindly rule
    Among the rustics there.

The chains by spells of beauty wove
    Grim time may soon dissever;
But she whose dower is her love
    Doth win the heart forever.
Soon, fondly plighted, we were wed
    In golden-leaf'd October.
The maples flamed, the sumac's red
    Blazed 'mid the russet sober.

Forth to the busy world we went,—
　　To floods of work and care,
Where waves leap high, where sails are rent,
　　Where danger haunts the air.
Our barque was tossed on heaving seas,
　　But safe each gale did ride.
We never lost our Port of Peace,
　　Our own dear ingleside.

When autumn rounded out the year,—
　　Because God loved us, maybe,—
There was another passenger,
　　A cooing, blue-eyed baby!
Oh, men! ye lose full half of life,
　　Its meaning and its blisses,
Who choose your lot *without a wife
　　Or baby's dewy kisses.*

Again our circle wider grew
　　For thee, my "little woman,"—
Room for another cherub, too.
　　Babes are the angels human.
Then o'er our hearts the shadow fell.
　　It was thy wing, O Death!
But since God doeth all things well,
　　We hush rebellious breath.

Ten blessed years 'mid joys and tears,
　　Sweetheart! let hope empower.
Here are our friends, whose presence cheers
　　And crowns this festal hour.
We thank you all. Our souls are full.
　　Heaven bless each kindly heart.
God help us make life beautiful,
　　And nobly do our part!

The Ministry of Grief.

[To a Mother bereaved of her first-born.]

THEY tell me he is dead!
That your sweet rosebud from the stem is torn,
The rarest jewel from your breast is borne,—
That at the fireside robbed you grieve and mourn,
    Your tender nestling fled.

    I know how sore your wo.
With anguish'd heartstrings wildly rent in twain,
In death's cold arms an only babe I've lain
Never to clasp that precious form again,
    Nor press those lips of snow.

    What hopes have paled apace!
For him a nobler life you would begin;
He should be wiser than you could have been,
Perhaps among earth's benefactors win
    A high and honored place.

    That blissful dream is o'er.
But since full many a snare lures tiny feet,
And now your darling treads the heavenly street,
And you've an angel child,—this is so sweet,
    You cannot murmur more.

    In truest love 't was done.
As when the shepherd from the dreary wold
Would lead the lingering flocks to summits bold,

His gentle arms an infant lamb enfold,
    Knowing 't will speed them on.

Through clouds God's mercy shines.
All suffering has a heaven-appointed use.
Some plants when trodden richer balm diffuse.
The shapeless block a patient sculptor hews
    To beauty's perfect lines.

Accept the seal of love.
The parent chastening proves his pity great.
Naught can befall by chance or sullen fate.
Griefs are veiled angels, that around us wait
    To wing the soul above.

Death opes the pearly door
To eyes that gaze submissively through tears.
Beyond the clamor of tempestuous fears,
Thy sainted one with beckoning smiles appears
    On heaven's resplendent shore.

Oh, most exceeding bliss!
There *lives* thy child, not lost, but *still thine own*.
By seraphs taught, more wise and noble grown.
Thou, too, by dainty baby hands art drawn
    To better worlds than this!

The Poet Awaiting a Verdict.

OUT on the restless ocean,
  The uncertain sea of life,
Amid the roar and motion
  Of business and of strife,
I cast my cherished bantlings,
  The children of my brain,
And wondered what their future
  Till they sail back again.

Those seabirds of my bosom,
  Trilling of love and home,-
Those creatures of my fancy,
  Now sent afar to roam.
Oh, what shall be their future?
  With flight sustained and strong,
To light on some fair islet,
  And charm the town with song?

Or, chilled and plumage ruffled,
  To sink where billows rave,
Their music caught and chanted
  By tuneful wind and wave?
Or, worse, quick home returning,
  No gift of song to find,
But tied around their dumb, sleek necks
  The luckless word, 'Declined?'

My Birds.

TIS said that when the Heavenly Child
   Had playful fashioned birds of clay,
Into the cold, mute forms he breathed,
And lo! they singing flew away!

Lord, I have wrought my birds with care.
   They will be lifeless without Thee.
Oh, breathe in them and in me breathe,
That both alive and tuneful be.

Violets.

SWEET Violets, your deep-blue eyes
    Almost bring tears into my own.
Ye waken childhood memories,
    Ye call back jocund days long flown.
I dream of Aprils, when, a maid
    I roamed the song-filled groves amid,
'Neath green-umbrella leaves of shade
    I found you " in poke-bonnets " hid,
Demure and modest, clad in blue,
The color dear to lovers true
A gaudier flower may charm the eye;
I prize your meek simplicity.
Upspringing 'neath the snow and rain,
You bravely lead the flowery train.
When Mother Earth receives my head,
Plant Violets upon my bed;
And say, with your unstudied art,—
' Who sleeps below gave all a part
Of that which was her best—her heart.'

www.ingramcontent.com/pod-product-compliance
Lightning Source LLC
Chambersburg PA
CBHW020827230426
43666CB00007B/1132